Love, Wine, and other Highs

ALSO BY LAUREN RAE

I'm Not a Writer

Love, Wine, and other Highs

a kind of memoir

Lauren Rae

Little
a

Published by Little A, New York

www.apub.com

Amazon, the Amazon logo, and Little A are trademarks of Amazon.com, Inc., or its affiliates.

ISBN-13: 9781542032360
ISBN-10: 1542032369

Cover design and illustration by Alyissa Letters

Internal illustrations by Alyissa Letters

Printed in the United States of America

To younger Lauren who never thought this possible,
this one is for you kiddo

PROLOGUE

Welcome to my brainchild.

A twenty-something babe with one goal in mind – to write in *any* capacity – I had to find a way to see it through, and that determination birthed this book.

It was always a dream of mine to create a book – one in which I could be completely myself – and I've scribbled all over the internet to fulfil that need to write, from my teens until today. When I was sixteen, my college professor told us we couldn't become successful writers without a blog, and so I took that as a personal challenge. Pouring my whole self into a blog aptly named 'The Shopaholics Anonymous', I posted weekly about not only my outfits, but also my failed attempts at dating and cringe stories heard via my friends. Using The Shopaholics Anonymous as my vision board, I learned that there was a market for my unique oversharing, and I greatly enjoyed subjecting potential boyfriends (lol) to the realm of no discretion. Then, what began as an online diary became a self-published piece of work, much of which is woven into this book. Yes, just like Carrie Bradshaw.

My first book, entitled *I'm Not a Writer*, felt like a leap into pretending to be a writer beyond my shoddily written blog posts. No longer shying away from people's questions of what I did for a living, working solo on this particular project felt like a step in the right direction, towards showing my newfound confidence. This self-deprecating piece of work, which detailed some of my most embarrassing life occurrences, was poorly written and yet, with the help of Ozlem Djafer's incredible artwork – perfectly designed – it was made slightly more bearable. The first step in rebuilding myself after a tumultuous breakup in 2018 with . . . let's call him John Doe 2, this seventy-two-page book comprised a series of personal essays detailing my anguish from a new point of view.

Taking my therapist's advice to write down my feels quite literally, *INAW* took shape and everything clicked for me, as I knew that an author was the very thing I'd always wanted to become. Debating between actually submitting my story or simply using the daily diary as a sounding board for my plethora of adult problems, I eventually bit the bullet and published my life story in 2019. And as I keep thinking to myself, if I had cowered, I might not be where I am today with *Love, Wine, and Other Highs*.

When I first toyed with the idea of writing a book – *INAW*, to be exact – I had no idea what its premise would be. All I knew was that I wanted to write something filled with whatever I wanted to write – and that it had to resonate with *me*, first and foremost. Having that first little memoir out in the world made me less ashamed of my growing list of personal red flags, and that was rather freeing. I considered the idea for at least two years before putting pen to paper, and while a number of my friends practically threatened me to get it out into the world, there was only one person's opinion that made me really want to create and eventually share that initial body of work with everybody. They say you may not always remember what people have said to you but you always remember how they made you feel, and that is true of this person.

Though it was a moment of great hurt and unforgettable angst, I'm eternally thankful to the individual who told me I should only write a book 'if it wasn't sad', because without you, I may never have had the confidence to put myself – my whole self – out there in this way. So thank you, John Doe 2, for breaking my heart when it was breakable, and for encouraging me to write not one but two books to rid myself of the heartache. No longer hurt or sad, I can say that your words are what helped to rebuild me. Having experienced what I can only describe as a near-death experience (or a breakup, whatever), I was able to hone in on and write down all my feelings in one specific place. Unable to leave my house for fear of bumping into John Doe 2 or any of his friends, writing this book became my safe space and I was able to unpack without raising any real concerns about my mental well-being. Although the first few drafts, which date back to 2018, are now safely stowed away in a trunk and dumped in the sea. Do not try to look for them.

Some of the chapters in *Love, Wine, and Other Highs* may read as sad, but what each chapter portrays is the rebirth of Lauren Rae, from the broken self of her childhood to the phoenix she slowly became from 2019. Now almost full and whole, I've used every ounce of hurt (and lols) throughout my life to create my love child: this book.

Admittedly, there are way too many *Sex and the City* references in this work, but similarly to Carrie in the season we wish we could forget, what started as a collection of my written work soon became a book.

Lauren Rae

RAE-LISATIONS

A list of notable quotables I've said and also considered putting on a T-shirt:

- 'GOT TIRED OF BEING A SAD BITCH, BACK TO BEING A BAD BITCH.'
- 'May the Ls [losses] I continue to take never take effect on my skin.'
- 'I fancy myself so much, I am my own MCM.'
- 'Ready to not be poor anymore.'
- 'She who braves a wax earns the right to show it off.'
- 'The secret to a happy life is listening to City Girls' "Act Up" and then Whitney Houston's "I'm Every Woman" on a constant loop.'
- 'I've hit my yearly quota for shooting my shot. Please contact the head office for further enquiries.'
- 'The first penis out of a relationship – remember you're falling for the penis, not the man. Don't be swayed by penis magic.'
- 'Spanx give me the waist I long desired but never acquired.'
- 'Equal rights – go get your dique wet!'
- 'POST BREAKUP WISDOM: it is what it is, what it is . . . what it is.'

- 'I can just tell this man wants to eat my pussy 'cause he keeps feeding me pineapple-based cocktails.'
- 'She's innovative. She's ambitious. She's tired.'
- 'I'm in love. How do I tell my FWB that I want to cut it back to two times a week?'
- 'And if you call me a BITCH, make sure you put AUTHOR in front of it.'
- 'This ponytail is longer than my life expectancy.'
- 'Don't think I'd have made it through the 1600s. How did they cope without vibrators?'
- 'I don't deserve to be poor.'
- 'My "person" is definitely on back order, because what the fuck is this?'
- 'Where there's a will, there's a wine.'
- 'Don't call it a takeover, call it a reluctance to return to social media and doing so anyways out of boredom.'
- 'My problem is I don't want someone unless they're obsessed with me, but I'm also icked by people who are obsessed with me.'
- 'I can't believe I ever had a "love of my life" when I am so clearly the love of my own life.'
- 'Uh-uh, baby, I am broker than my mental health.'
- 'Pretending to have my life together is much more fun than *actually* getting it together.'
- 'Really liking someone is a level of vulnerability I'm unequipped for tbh.'
- 'I knew I was having a hard time getting through my breakup when I couldn't rewatch *X-Men* because of its title.'
- 'I'm only focused on two things: my craft and my clitoris.'
- 'Commitments with buyouts = friends with benefits.'
- 'I rode that face like it was my last train home.'

The Writer & her Childhood Traumas

Chapter 1: The Writer & Her Childhood Traumas

Isn't it ironic that the power of manifestation is supposedly real, yet none of my M.A.S.H. life predictions came to fruition?

In my formative years, I was certain that growing up meant I'd eventually get married to Lee from Blue, own an English bulldog and live lavishly in a six-bedroom house in Notting Hill with no financial worries. It was quite literally written in the cards for me. Well, by 'cards' I mean on a piece of paper in a game of M.A.S.H., where the process of elimination determined my future marriage, home and career path.

By contrast, my childhood (and subsequently my coming-of-age story) often felt like the black version of a Jacqueline Wilson novel. I spent many of my prepubescent years invested in the tumultuous lives of her characters, and my life as a child of divorce seemed to slot right in to her books about broken children and broken homes. Wilson's novels were my favourite form of escapism, used as a distraction from my nomad-like, house-hopping, post-divorce existence. My interest in reading and fictional characters helped to expand my world view, and encouraged me to adopt an optimistic attitude towards my *real*-life problems.

Strong enough to leave a marriage that was no longer serving her, my mother moved on with my brother and me in tow. Though I was only a sprog at the time, I understood the severity of the situation, thanks to being bold enough to watch late-night viewings of *EastEnders* through the crack in the living-room door. With a single TV donated by one of our family members, a white hospital blanket and a handful of Iceland snacks, we moved on from a large family home in Kenton to an apartment complex in Harrow – the first step to becoming a new family. What was initially an empty canvas soon filled with post-divorce memorabilia, by way of individual TVs with backoffs for my older brother and I, scratched CDs that meant a ruined listening experience, and umpteen Disney movies on VHS. We were home.

Moving on from the problem of where my parents would meet to hand over the kids to whose turn it was to watch cable come 6 p.m. on the front-room TV, I watched as my mother rebuilt her life as a single woman, and I began to look at her as something of an inspiration – in the same way I did with the characters in my favourite novels. Her tenacity, in addition to her stunning good looks, ignited something in me from very early on. She rocked knee-high heeled boots, a cropped Kelly Rowland haircut, and slim-fitting outfits that accentuated her figure, but she was more than just her perfect appearance. While I envied her good looks and wondered if I'd ever grow up to be as peng as she was (is), I also adopted an 'I can do it on my own' attitude at a young age by watching her brave approach to single motherhood.

Aside from my love of Blockbuster rentals, frequent rereads of Jaqueline Wilson's *Midnight* and writing anonymous love letters to my crushes, sleepovers were my childhood activity of choice, but with these came their own set of rules. There was no stress greater than that of standing hand-in-hand with my bestie at her house, asking my mother if I could stay the night. Now, I often liken my stress levels to how I felt with regard to one of two situations: 1) shaving my head in an attempt to restore some semblance of control, and 2) asking to sleep over at a friend's house when my mother had already arrived to pick me up. There is absolutely no in between.

My friend and I would spend our last allotted hour together, trying to devise a plan for how to approach the situation. *Do we ask together? Do I volunteer my friend as tribute and make her ask so that my mother can't say no? Do we hold hands, and attack with cutesy?* Ultimately, we were setting up a PowerPoint presentation before we even knew what PowerPoint was, with all the pros and cons as to why I should be allowed to stay the night at my mate's house – totally inconveniencing my mother, might I add. Little did we know we were merely training for the hours of intense networking and self-selling to come.

Now, the reason I always liken my stress levels to these two situations in particular is simple, but I'll explain a little more for those at the back. In the case of head-shaving – well, it's pretty obvious that hitting this stress level means code motherfucking red. When I reach this point, there's absolutely no saving the situation. It's hopeless. Every terrible thing that has happened to me since the age of four plays in my head as though death is nigh. But at this point I've come to appreciate this for its cinematic beauty – in the brief periods when I can actually catch my breath. The teenhood rejections; being called a turd by my Year 6 crush; accidentally eating a dog biscuit and being bitten by said dog; sitting on chewing gum and ruining my favourite trousers in middle school; my first boyfriend and my inability to talk to him once there was a label in place. All of it.

In my head, because my mother did usually allow me to spend my weekends and after-school hours frolicking with my friends in their respective homes, everyone else's must've done so too. So when I liken the second stress level to asking to stay at a friend's house, I just assume everyone's been through the stressful process of asking – and the potential of being rejected – and somehow gotten their way every now and then. Both a blessing and a curse, the experience prepared me for the future. If not for me asking my mother to lug an overnight bag with an extra pair of undies and possibly my school uniform over to Edgware from the depths of Harrow, I likely wouldn't be able to ask the questions most people are fearful of, whether that's 'Dude, are you into me or not?' or 'Are you gonna eat your Monster Munch?' while gluttonously staring at the unopened purple packet.

NAPPILY NEVER AFTER

As a child, nothing was more damaging than my relationship with my hair. Though I was determined to love it – and in turn, love myself – there was a small part of me that wanted to shave it all off and cover my scalp with someone else's hair. Never privy to 'I love your hair' comments, I felt slightly short-changed in having hair that everyone complained about combing. It led me to only feel comfortable if my hair was hidden beneath the braids my mother spent two nights styling, and wash day always filled me with unmitigated dread. To this day, I still struggle to let my hair loose in its natural state in front of anyone who isn't related to me or my best friend.

I've since come to the harsh realisation that the reason for my tumultuous relationship with my hair is the running commentary on it in my formative years. From older family members likening my tresses to sheep's wool, to having referred to it as 'tough' while in the detangling process, I came to see my hair the way everyone else did – as nothing more than a burden. While my mother's hair cascaded down to her shoulders and grew a mile a minute, my own would barely clear my ears, and I resented my follicles for it. Unable to grow what the natural hair community would regard as 'healthy hair', my self-esteem only worsened as everything grew in puberty except the hair on my head. I ignored comments that brought me to tears later, when I was alone, and wondered why I was cursed with this thing that everyone – myself included – hated.

Learning to mask my insecurities with flowing ponytails and styles that hid as much of my natural hair as possible, I later became very good at doing my own hair from the comfort of my own home. A dab hand with a half wig, a fine-tooth comb and a pair of straighteners, I mastered how to make synthetic hair look as though it was growing from my scalp, and began to hear compliments that boosted my confidence. Rather than dwelling on my inability to grow natural hair that reached my chest, I instead focused on *pretending* that I could.

Though we're now told we should love and appreciate our hair in its natural state, it's something I know quite a few people still struggle with – and this is often because of the trauma of being bullied about it at a young age. I was made fun of for my hair being 'picky' and routinely asked why it was so short, and these statements echoed in my brain any time I dared to wear my hair out. It wasn't until the age of twenty-three that I was comfortable having my hair straightened and worn out without the comfort of my extensions. I lived in fear of anyone commenting on my natural hair when they eventually saw it.

4C hair, though I'm now learning to love it, hasn't always been the easiest of rides. Never seeing myself represented in the magazines I forced my mother to subscribe to was hard. Unable to participate in *Mizz* magazine hairstyles, I spent the entirety of my Sunday evenings perched between my mother's legs as she prepared my hair for the week. Butterfly clips were saved for truly special occasions, and not for the sixty-second style tips given unto us via teen magazines. I felt excluded as my classmates paraded round school with new looks directly sourced from our favourite mags, which further contributed to my growing disdain for my locks.

Why couldn't I tie my hair up into an obnoxious side pony, or show off the quick hacks I tore out of magazines and stuck on my wall?

Though I hate to admit it, many of the magazines I subscribed to contributed to the way that I viewed myself growing up. I was mortified to discover that my school friends washed their hair every day, rather than every four weeks, and envied how easy it was for them with their wash-and-go technique. Subscribing to the ideal of more manageable hair, my hair was relaxed in Year 6. But in what was a stale attempt at finally fitting in with my white counterparts, my limp tresses felt more like a betrayal of my natural hair than a help for those styling it. As my hair lost its lustre and flattened against my scalp, the burning sensation of the relaxer felt like a huge price for such a small pay-out.

The damaging commentary surrounding my hair always felt like I shouldn't have been in the room to hear it, whether it was family members saying that my hair was like sheep's wool or the hairdresser telling me that my hair would need to be relaxed in order for them to deal with it. Any of my attempts to salvage my natural hair were met with mockery and disdain, and so I gave in to the peer pressure and relaxed it again, and again, and again.

Sure, I was able to tie it up into a bun without the added help of a headscarf, but at what cost? The DIY kits meant that my now dry hair soon lost all its nutrients and needed more care and attention than my untouched, natural hair. Relaxing my hair at such a young age also reinforced the idea that its natural state just wasn't good enough, and set a dangerous precedent that would see me hate my natural hair more and more as time ticked on. I wasn't uplifted by the abundance of black hair profiles seen today, and YouTube videos on how to style your hair (and avoid the comments heard in the stylist's chair) weren't a thing. Admittedly, I'm jealous of the next generation, who will be taught to love their natural coils from the very beginning, as years of being told otherwise have left scars on both my scalp and my self-esteem.

Solange was once quoted as saying that, without her weave, she felt unnoticeable and unpretty, and that's something that's always stuck with me. (There will be enough Solange references to last a lifetime in this memoir.) Seeking comfort in content about learning to love my hair, I've been inspired by the 'Don't Touch My Hair' singer. Constantly changing her tresses to suit her style, Solange has been instrumental in reminding me that my hair is my own and I can do with it what I please.

Nowadays, I feel like a brand-new person after getting my hair done, and for me there's something truly special about the chair at the hairdresser's. Entering with the spirit of a basic and leaving with that of a bad bitch, the transformative effect of each braid is nothing short of magic.

THE PRE-RIHANNA EFFECT

Before Rihanna and her many inspirational haircuts, there lived the 2000s British teen. With a solid sense of self, these trendsetters cared little for how stupid they might look and instead started something of a movement in hair.

From dramatically side-swept ponytails and detailed cane-row styles, to slicked edges that reached the slope of your brow and backcombed poufs, the real trendsetters were those who experimented with their tresses. Having experienced every hair phase, I think of myself as something of an expert. As a teenager testing out who I might become as an adult via my ever-changing hairstyles, I greatly enjoyed trialling styles that might not necessarily have suited me but felt one step closer to the person I would become. Influenced by Paramore and System of a Down while simultaneously being obsessed with *Frank* by Amy Winehouse and the latest Tinchy Stryder hit played promptly at 6 p.m. on Channel U, my hairstyles changed more than my friends' teen relationships. Spoiler: there were a lot of teen relationships.

Pre-Rihanna's *Good Girl Gone Bad*, many of my weekends were spent slumped between my best friend's legs while she attempted new styles she thought might look cute on me. Our frequent trips to the local Pak's and our dedication to keeping up with the times meant we had our own little hair salon. From perming just our edges so we could slick them easily, to cutting full fringes under dim lighting – no dream was too far out of our reach, despite our limited resources.

When I glance at school kids in clusters at the bus stop today, it's with disbelief. A far cry from my own teen experience, they're completely skipping the embarrassing fashion faux pas that helped us to develop a sense of style later on in life, and I'm almost a little jealous. Wearing muted tones and drawing their brows on correctly for the era they're living through, apps and websites like TikTok and YouTube have completely robbed young people of the early phase of looking completely stupid. I look at the teens of today and wonder if skipping this questionable rite of passage will affect them later in life, enabling them to acquire high self-esteem earlier than they should. Okay, now I'm really jealous.

For those of you who grew up in an era that favoured colour-co-ordinated laces and lollipops strategically placed in side ponytails, you might sit and ponder what the teens of today will have to look back on and chuckle at when scouring through memories in photograph form. Us 2000s teens are scarred by the memory of wearing concealer on our lips, while Gen Z can go through life knowing that they never once looked like the victim on an episode of *CSI*. They'll avoid entirely the make-up routines that made us look like extras from *Big Fat Gypsy Weddings*, when our Maybelline mascara efforts were more 'Can you tell I'm wearing MASCARA?!' than 'Oh these? They're just my natural lashes x'.

Using the tips handed to me via Sabrina the Teenage Witch's magazine *Sabrina's Secrets*, my efforts were in vain as each edition, more expensive than the last – due to its additional 'free' accessories – meant that make-up looks encompassed an excessive amount of glitter and brightly coloured eyeshadow palettes. Frankly, I was doomed from the very beginning.

Magazines such as *Mizz* and *Bliss* were all about body glitter, butterfly clips and lavish embellishments – and so, despite not being their target audience, I wanted to be too. But in their step-by-step picture format, the make-up tips felt more like *Art Attack*'s 'Here's one I made earlier' and were far harder to understand than the guided YouTube tutorials of the present day. Somewhat of a helping hand, but perhaps more a guide in what *not* to do, these teen magazines showed me how to emulate my favourite celebrities. We could all look like Ashley Tisdale at the premiere of *Ice Princess* . . . if, of course, we looked exactly like Ashley Tisdale with her iconic blonde tresses in the first place.

These magazines unintentionally excluded black teens like myself, and so instead we used the black hair magazines stacked in hair shops for inspiration. Circling the styles I wished to try – as I did with toys I wanted in the Argos catalogue – I begged my parents to let the stylist flat-iron my hair, narrowly avoiding moderate ear and scalp burns in the process. All in a bid to look like the beautiful unnamed model featured on the cover of *Black Beauty* and imitate the butterfly-clipped styles featured in teen magazines dominated by white faces.

Media-wide, icons such as Lady Sovereign (whose hit 'Love Me or Hate Me' still low-key slaps) are key visuals when describing what growing up at that time might have looked like. Despite a modest amount of cultural appropriation, Sovereign's style – including obnoxious side ponytails and graphic printed T-shirts – was a sign of the times for British teenagers. A great example of what most of us looked like for a period of time, her loud colour coordination could appear in history textbooks to illustrate one of the seven pillars of 2000s teen fashion in the UK. In retrospect, our outlandish need to wear *all* of the colours at once and be *seen* by all our Myspace friends is likely the cause of today's muted Instagram feeds and rampant social anxiety, but I digress.

As a black teen, there was the added allure of trialling new and experimental cane-row styles, much to the dismay of teachers who had little understanding of expressing yourself through hair. Adding flare to an otherwise simple black staple, attempts at detailed cane-row styles reigned in the early noughties and certainly throughout my own high-school years. Often styled by friends who were certain they'd own their own salons in the future, a criss-cross here and a map to Terabithia there, combined with soggily gelled edges, meant that poses with our phones above our heads and a tilted angle were the only viable option. Fusing our individuality with the fast-changing times, these styles helped preteens like myself to develop which styles were suited to their head shape – in addition to competing for the most creative look.

Having our hair styled by friends and family members after school, the road to self-expression began early for a few of us as we trialled new styles – with the added worry of whether or not we might be expelled for doing so. It was experimental and exciting, and were you really living if you weren't traipsing through Primark looking for the perfect shade of purple laces to wear in your hair . . . and also in one of your school shoes? These styles were quite different – and questionable, to be frank – but oh, to be a part of UK Urban history. Each of these small factors contributed to our individuality and style and also the way we each navigate our individual style today, as we reference many of the looks we served as teens – although on a slightly smaller scale.

FASHION FAUX,
NO SHE BETTER DON'T

These tiny fashion moments in our teenscape influenced the way we behave today. When asked why I don't wear colour and instead opt for a quieter closet of black on black with a little bit of black for pizzazz, I shudder and remember the occasion I wore six different shades of purple in one outfit simply because they 'matched'. Then I simply respond with: 'This is just who I am now.' British teens in the early 2000s looked vastly different than teens today, with our choice of pose almost *moderately* offensive. Our hunched backs and bent knees (to fit the entire ensemble in a photo) are likely the cause of our poor posture as adults.

I remember receiving evil looks the first time I walked into college wearing Levi's shorts and Effy-from-*Skins* tights (both ripped), knee-high grey socks and washed black desert boots. It was the first time post-high school that I'd used my own money to buy my own clothes – from Primark, Topshop, New Look et al. – in a stale attempt to tie all of my personalities into one look.

What this period in my life showed me was that many people were terrified of individuality and instead hoped we'd all be boxed into the same trope of bedazzled jeggings, Ugg boots and oversized off-the-shoulder sweater . . . with a Paul's Boutique bag. But I dabbled in trialling all styles, and greatly enjoyed the duality of reaching each extreme.

Figuring out myself through fashion and what it meant to be comfortable in my own style, I was rarely fearful of pushing the boundaries with my outfits at college, but I was definitely fearful of the backlash. Often referred to as a 'Bounty' because I didn't tick all the boxes of what it meant to be black, I was open to blurring the lines and adopting fashions from wherever I saw inspiration. Emulating the hairstyles of my black counterparts while picking up fashion tips from my white peers, I was trying to test the boundaries and find myself very early in my teen years. Of course this also meant a discourse as to why I had both Lady Gaga and Donell Jones on my iPod Shuffle.

I recall my mother being quite terrified of this phase, as I'm certain she thought it meant I'd take up smoking cigarettes and snorting various drugs, but I was more interested in discovering what best suited me . . . and maybe trialling WKD with my friends, if that even counts?

Nowadays, with the help of apps like Instagram and Pinterest, there's little excuse for us to be dressed poorly, as there is always some form of inspiration to hand. However, back then, Disney shows and MTV Base music video premieres were my main source of inspiration, varying from midriff-focused ensembles to *13 Layers Why*. I'm often haunted by the memory of when flowy skirts paired with bedazzled bootcut jeans and holey ponchos were a thing on the red carpet. A thing that was allowed, and also scored via 'who wore it best' percentages on how . . . good it looked. Our own version of a world war, in fashion, many of our fast-fashion options have since been made redundant, with no chance of a revival. Thank goodness.

A perfect example is none other than Raven-Symoné at the premiere of *Pirates of the Caribbean: The Curse of the Black Pearl*. Encompassing the entirety of the noughties with one red-carpet look, her monochromatic outfit was accented by a covetable small Louis Vuitton bag (which cost about the same as my rent today) and light-tinted sunglasses that dominated my fashion fantasies. On the cooler side of noughties fashion, her outfit was fashion inspo for many of us, and we tried to emulate it via the 'Everything £10' stores found up and down the local high street, with off-the-shoulder tops and brightly coloured bra straps we had no business wearing. Our attempt to copy this particular look meant that Primark stocks went through the roof, as it was the only store where we could find the right kind of flared skirt with *that* grey stripe on the waistband.

Substituting old fashion personas for all-new ones via an evolving wardrobe, I stressed my parents out as it meant them forking out cash each time I changed my mind even slightly. My parents were likely worried about each of the drastic phases I went through as they grappled with the ever-changing landscape of teen fashion: faux-pearl necklaces, jeggings, almost transparent leggings, 3D cinema glasses with the lenses poked out, and a variety of questionable waist belts – with an honourable mention for the boho circle belt that showed no discrimination towards its wearers, as it was adjustable to fit all. Most notable was the neon phase that was shared by so many adolescents. My mind has apparently blocked this from my memory in full – and rightly so, as the images that do appear in my brain from time to time, via a rudimentary 'lol remember when you looked like dis' slideshow, are nothing short of embarrassing. The perfect U18 club attire involved being seen from any part of the dimly lit Oceana dance floor, as neon tights, tops and accessories were totally and completely a thing. I shudder at the thought.

Transitioning from a quirky young teen to college attendee meant that it was time to rid myself of the brightly coloured ensembles and instead turn my attention to faux-Ugg boots (until I got a part-time job at Claire's and made enough to upgrade to the real thing). Typically worn with ageing bobbly jeggings from one of the fifteen £5 shops near me, and accessorised with beaded necklaces, a keffiyeh scarf and layered cardigans, is it any wonder my mother was concerned about the questionable outfits I wore on my pointless group trips to the Apple Store in Brent Cross?

I can attribute the ample number of colourful, printed Kai Collective pieces that my closet overflows with today to dressing like a total wallad in my teens. For the moments where I'm feeling particularly colourful. Those lessons in pattern-clashing and colour-blocking to the nth degree definitely paved the way for many of my current fashion choices, but I do hope that, one day, all-purple outfits inspired by 1980s workout gear will make a much-needed third return, so that brightly coloured leg warmers can once again lead the charge.

OH, TO BE A MEMBER OF THE MIDRIFF SOCIETY

Britney Spears was a leading member of the midriff society that dominated in the 1990s and early 2000s, along with Janet Jackson, Christina Aguilera and Mariah Carey, to name just a few. They were the crew in charge of pairing tiny crop tops with low-rise jeans that would nearly show their nether regions. With the media dominated by unachievable abs, little girls the world over tied up our tops while attempting the 'I'm a Slave 4 U' choreography that left us sweating in our character-themed pyjamas.

Despite our adoration of the likes of Christina Aguilera, who donned a scarf and belt-skirt with all the confidence of a middle-aged white man, for many of us this was a turning point in our growing body insecurities. Watching beautiful women writhing in sweat next to medium-ugly men was a confusing time for those of us shaped like a Nokia 6300. Although we gyrated with the same vigour as the video vixens featured in 'Thong Song', we were concerned that our prepubescent bodies hadn't yet sprung the right amount of breastage to slow-motion jiggle.

Even while carrying out the sage advice given in Judy Blume's *Are You There, God? It's Me, Margaret*, I could not in fact increase my bust, and so I used the quick-fix method of stuffing my make-shift crop top with balled-up pairs of socks instead. An act that would precede the only time my father gave me inaccurate advice, which was: 'They will grow in eventually!' They never did. And that's just the tip of the iceberg. I was mocked for 'at least' being skinny, and my own brand of body insecurity is riddled with guilt for not loving a body I'm routinely told I should be lucky to have.

The thought 'I've got no idea what I actually look like' rings truer every time, and doubts about my body have done a real number on me over the years. As an 'acceptable' size, I've come to terms with the fact that perhaps slim is my aesthetic. But I've had a difficult relationship with my body, and being slim hasn't always felt like the blessing I've often been told it is.

Dating in my early teens posed new insecurities in relation to my physique. My partners often joked about my slim stature and having 'nothing to grab on to' during sweaty make-out sessions. Dating is its own fresh hell, but these comments led me to put a lot of my self-worth into what men thought of me – especially as I already thought myself undesirable. Appeasing the male gaze led me to wear baggier clothes, so as not to invite comments about my bony and 'lanky' stature. And my preferred mufti-day clothing went from skinny three-quarter-length trousers to Champion jogging bottoms and a Le Coq Sportif sweatshirt.

Trapped in my own head, reaching out to friends and family members only added fuel to the fire – as my dislike of my small bodily defects was dismissed. Layers helped to avoid questions about whether or not I was starving myself, and deterred conversations about my gluttonous eating habits on the off chance I allowed myself to eat in front of new people.

In middle school, my classmates and I selected our body types via a chart that determined whether you were Straight, Slim, Curvy, etc., and even in recalling this memory I understand how this contributed to the issue. We each chose the body type we believed represented us most, and when I listed my pick of 'Slim', I was mocked by everyone and compared to a number of flat surfaces. Which, okay, isn't the worst thing in the world to happen. But as a twelve-year-old kid with no real understanding of what I actually looked like, my belief system in the mirrors I peered into was shaken.

In the black community, slimness isn't necessarily an aspirational trait. In fact, it's usually quite the opposite. I felt less than, because I wasn't curvaceous like my family members said I'd be by age eighteen. Frequently being told in my home country of Barbados that I was built like a coat hanger only further contributed to my wanting to be covered up all the time, so as not to attract attention or comments about my body.

I was mocked for not having breasts (which still makes no sense to me, because all the women in my family do!!!!!), berated for not having a J.Lo bottom, and jested with for not developing hips. Despite this being infinitely different to fatphobia – and, of course, incomparable – each comment over the years has had me questioning how I feel about my figure when I look in the mirror and chipped away at my self-esteem. Much like Mulan in the epic Disney flick, I too questioned who the girl staring back at me in the mirror was.

I began to wonder how and where my quirky brand of beauty would fit in – and I constantly pitted myself against the perfect-skinned beauties I saw on MTV. Holding on to these insecurities – which partly stemmed from watching the latest music videos from artists like 50 Cent – I struggled as my distorted view of my frame followed me into adulthood. I often question if the stream of suggested posts appearing in between the photos from friends and celebrities I follow is Instagram's sneaky little way of suggesting that I augment my own reality by way of surgery. I also wonder if this marketing ploy is the reason why so many of us are sucked in. Changing my hair on a monthly and sometimes weekly basis, the high can only last for so long, because when I log in to post my slay online, I'm met with an onslaught of women who are naturally much prettier and trimmer than I am. Even with my jazzy new hairstyle that grants me the perfect facelift.

Constantly comparing myself to others when simply browsing the net is incredibly hard to distance myself from, as there's no real escape. Even if you choose not to follow the Bella Hadids of the world, they still somehow find their way into your suggested posts to remind you that you might be hot, but you'll never be Bella frickin' Hadid.

Then there are the hours spent critiquing my frame after seeing the cinched waists and beautiful bottoms sprawled all over my 'Explore' page. Despite always sharing my figure online when I feel a surge in dopamine, it's as a confidence boost for myself as opposed to being for the instant gratification of others, and my self-esteem falls flat when I'm reminded of all the passing comments on my frame up to now.

> *I know I'm *supposed* to love my figure, but I spend 90% of the day hating it and the other 10% taking photos that say otherwise.*

—@lawrenrae_, making absolute sense.

Many of the societal pressures placed on teens originate with social media via influencers and celebrities, in addition to TV, movies and magazines – not to mention the patriarchy through the centuries. And each of these sources contributes to a growing brand of insecurities about our bodies. The wheels spin a mile a minute, with images churned out on social media – and teenagers are bombarded by these images at an alarming rate. Comparing ourselves to these unobtainable faces and figures helps to distort our own reality, as even when we roll our eyes at airbrushed photos, we still wish to reach those unrealistic beauty standards.

When I was younger, it felt a little easier to shut out the pressures placed on women to look a certain way, by turning off the TV or throwing your glossy magazines in the bin. While there were those of us who practically starved ourselves in the hopes of emulating Kate Moss's figure, today's equally dangerous beauty standards feel harder to distance ourselves from – as there's no 'off' switch in today's incredibly switched-on culture.

In the 2010s the 'Insta baddie' aesthetic appeared from the ashes with one mission and one mission only: to make us question everything about our appearance. Often consisting of a perfectly plump pout, a Kim K-like figure and stakes in Fashion Nova, the rise of the Insta baddie meant the loss of our self-esteem.

We've sort of been conditioned to believe our original form isn't good enough in comparison to our perfectly filtered peers. As we became less fixated on looking like the stick figures strutting down runways in couture, we just chose a new body type to obsess over – fixating on the equally unattainable figures constructed through dangerous surgeries. Our preoccupation with half of the cast of *Love & Hip Hop* left us questioning if perhaps we'd be better with a real-life filter or two.

A beloved game of mine, in which you pretend a simulated life is your real one, is Sims 4, and Instagram's influence was also reflected in my characters. By accentuating their features in ways people do IRL – by way of the famed BBL (Brazilian butt lift) and breast augmentations – my Sims were afforded modifications I maybe couldn't summon up the costs for in the real world, and I created whole new personas via these 2020 versions of my online characters. It's low-key worrying when you realise how deeply obsessed we are with this vision of a new reality.

In true Y2K fashion, famed shows like *That's So Raven* and *Lizzie McGuire* tried to help us navigate the difficult conversations surrounding weight, albeit not always successfully. In the former, Raven Baxter's otherwise-bubbly onscreen personality stepped aside during one of my favourite episodes, which highlighted a major issue with the fashion industry at the time: the revering of the size-zero model. In this episode, Raven, known primarily for her quirky choices in fashion, is competing for a chance to become the next big thing in design. On a mission to become the same size as the model assigned to her, Raven is set on a dangerous course towards negative thoughts about her figure, as she is challenged on her vision of being both model for her own designs *and* designer.

Similarly, the hit show *Lizzie McGuire* included one of the few depictions of an eating disorder we were able to see as preteens, and demonstrated how tough misperceptions of the self can be when growing up. After seeing a Polaroid photograph of herself, Lizzie's best friend Miranda is mortified, quickly becoming obsessed with her weight, and so she begins a torrid relationship with food. It was a darker story than was usual for Disney's typically happy-go-lucky programming, and the episode and Miranda's journey resonated with me deeply – as I too felt like eating was the only aspect of my teenage life I could control.

NOT ANOTHER TEEN TRAUMA

Being an unattractive teen was a fucking trip – well, at least for me, as it would take years for me to finally grow into my face and other boob – as I only had one for the majority of my teen years. We were subject to extensive ridicule because of the hairstyles we thought were cool, the oversized school clothes our parents swore blind we'd grow into, and the constant rotation of friendships – usually due to teen pregnancy, fallouts over new boyfriends, and a general resentment towards one another that grew over the years. Had we known we'd carry these awkward atrocities with us into adulthood, we'd have likely slowed our roll on the YOLO moments and faced our books instead.

I understand that many of the things I dislike about myself are because of comments I was unable to shake off while growing up. I was routinely told that my nose was 'pig-like', and my granddad tried to slim it by pinching it every day. The things I hated most were always focal points for my peers. Though I'd likely never do anything to change them, out of pure fear of Michael Jacksoning my face, my hatred for these attributes has only grown over time, and when I'm at my lowest, I only see those talking points staring back at me. My pig-shaped nose still haunts me, and I do everything I can with my hair and angles to make it seem less dominating in the centre of my face.

In my teen years I was heavily reliant on developing a personality, as I was far and away behind the others in looks. I rocked beaten-up Kickers school shoes with colourful laces, although they would never conceal my buck teeth, which my dentist said were developing 'as they were supposed to'. I turned to my all-black school uniform to add some flare and pizzazz to an otherwise blank canvas, and drew attention to my shortened tie and my school trousers tucked into the tongues of my shoes to distract from the acne on my forehead and my single barely-an-A-cup boob.

Through the bullying I experienced at high school, I became accustomed to being sad. Many of us misremember where our internet personalities *actually* began, but for my generation the reality is developed via a barrage of 'Who's Hotter – X or Y?' polls on Piczo. Before our migration to Facebook friend lists and Myspace Top 8s, any free time after school was spent refreshing our Piczo pages minute after minute, typing in the URL address www.babyfacecutiepengness.piczo.com and damaging our sight looking at pages with one too many rotating gifs.

This was just the beginning of our low self-esteem issues online. With our introduction to the internet came its own trendier brand of cruelty, and the baby trolls sat behind their Windows 95-style keyboards. Our need to judge a person by attacking their appearance came long before Instagram – if you're old enough to remember refreshing the twinkly page to make sure your votes were level with your opponents on the dreaded 'Hot or Not' list. The fucking horror. Soon it'd all be over, and it would be someone else's turn to be judged on their adolescent appearance. And although you knew the horror, you still complied with the rules of the online coven and casted your vote. Baby trolls in the making. Your innocent adolescence pitted against someone else's full development meant questioning why you hadn't been granted the same timeline for puberty.

Youth was hardly a picnic, and even if you thought you were cute, someone was ready to test this logic by putting your name beside theirs on the interwebs and taking you down a peg or two. Step one to self-hate. Had I known the lasting effects of the internet, I might've committed to an offline vocation. While many claim not to have known how much early examples of social media were fucking us up as youths, it seems almost naïve looking back, as it's heavily contributed to my withering self-esteem.

A late developer, I watched as the chests of the other girls in my class began to enlarge, and was mocked for not yet having one. Creepy as that may sound – simply put, I was envious, as my development felt as slow as my ability to see when a guy wasn't interested. Each day in Year 8 the news broke of someone else starting their period, and I feared that perhaps my day would just never come. I knew very little about periods other than the fact they involved blood, your private parts, and other variables my peers and I embarrassingly giggled about during Sex Ed. But given that my friends and I had gone through many of the same bodily changes at the same time – growth spurts, new teeth and joint pain – I felt cheated that I didn't get to scream about a drop of blood staining my Groovy Chick underpants along with them. Waiting ever so impatiently, I begged my mother to at least take me bra shopping, so I could experience what it really meant to go through puberty like my peers. Though I wish we'd waited, because my chest barely filled an A-cup and the straps felt more like a Victorian-age corset than one step closer to feeling like a young woman.

Convinced that my day was nigh, I remixed Judy Blume's famed quote about increasing the bust to reference my period, and crossed my fingers waiting for the moment my own Red Sea would part. But despite my efforts, I was still months behind my counterparts, and when it did finally arrive, I wished the chant of 'I must, I *must* begin my period' hadn't worked as well as it did.

Typically, children of divorce are made to split their time between both parents, and so I spent every other weekend at my father's home in North West London. As usual, I had my head buried in one of Jacqueline's latest plots, but something about this weekend felt different. Reading *Girls in Love*, I sat with my legs hanging over the arm of my nana's new leather sofa, much to her dismay. On one of my scheduled bathroom breaks – which I only awarded myself after finishing a new chapter – I scurried to the bathroom, where I discovered it: my first period. Terrified, excited and numb, in that moment I remembered my whereabouts, and I was forced to get creative with Andrex toilet tissue. After fashioning my first emergency pad, I ran to my Siemens A55 mobile phone and used the 'emergency only' credit to call my mum and demand that she get in the car because *it* had just happened. Too scared to utter the words to my father, there I stood – a newly developed thirteen-year-old kid – in his bathroom, with my bloodstained bottoms and tissue poking out of my underpants. Patiently, I waited for the obnoxious-sounding doorbell to ring, and for my mum to hand me whatever tools I needed to absorb the bleeding.

This was just a segue into a multitude of awkward occurrences to come, as learning the ins and outs of periods (beyond the excitement of actually having one) meant understanding the teenage mood swings I'd only seen via my favourite onscreen characters. While I was shedding my uterine lining, I was around my father who hadn't a clue how to navigate this either – and so we began to drift further apart. The wall between us grew higher and higher, graffitied with a list of things we couldn't talk about, and many of those were lady-specific problems.

Despite finally getting my period and starting to feel more 'womanly' or whatever, nothing really changed. I was still hideous to look at – probably more so by that point, as my forehead had pus-filled tenants. I led with humour, and quickly asserted myself as one of the boys' girls because I knew that they would have no interest in me; and given my obsession with Chr*s Br*wn and Omarion at the time, they weren't even in my peripherals anyway. Still a Year 8er, I soon became the best of friends with Adam, who saw me beyond my ill-fitting facial features and terrible teeth. Bantering about random shit that happened at school, we'd spend after-school hours switching between conversations on MSN Messenger and SMS, and glittering each with emoticons. But as glossy as this new-found friendship felt, it was just a turd in disguise, as his girlfriend didn't take kindly to it. My introduction to real bullying – as it didn't stop there – seems almost pathetic when looking back, because it all began over a boy I had zero interest in courting.

Cornering me on my lunch break, the Year 9 girls who were friends with Adam's girlfriend felt it necessary to tell me to back off from him. So, I cried. I envy the lack of shame I had at thirteen, because in the present day I might've composed myself, saved it, and burst into tears in one of the bathroom stalls. However, back then I waited for all of forty-five seconds of stuttering 'We . . . we're *jus*— just friends . . .' before I let my cheeks flood with tears. I had never been confronted in this way before, and certainly not over a boy. This new and foreign territory set a dangerous precedent, as I was subjected to more of the same in the high-school years that followed. Even when Adam's girlfriend didn't say it, her friends made sure to give me a sharp look to keep me away from hanging out with Adam – whether alone or in a group of five.[1]

---

1   I mean, eventually they broke up and he ended up with me, so she was probably right to worry, BUT WE DIDN'T PLAN THAT!!!
† *Dead creps* – terrible footwear.

Growing up as what the K*rdashians might refer to as 'poor' was no easy feat. While brands like Reebok and Le Coq Sportif may reign supreme now, back in the day wearing them was a masterclass in how to be mocked for the entirety of the school year. Pulling out your 'dead creps'[†] while getting ready for a lesson of running and sweating was step one in becoming the focal point, and a few of us still hold some form of resentment towards affordable sneakers. In fact, I'm haunted by the time my trainers loudly and grotesquely smacked the ground during the dreaded bleep test. This was the beginning of me being boxed in by what other people thought of my style choices, despite me not actually being able to do anything about them. My PE kit was always the least of my worries, as my attention was turned to which Primark embellishment would make my school uniform pop for the other four and a half hours spent at school. Alas, those of us who donned Reebok Classics succumbed to jeers about our social class and our parents' income – which, when looking back, is kind of terrible.

But I credit my beaten-up Reebok creps with me meeting my friend Kizzle for the first time. We locked eyes across the sports hall and smiled at each other. She immediately took to me, scurrying over during our allotted thirty minutes of cardio in our matching grey and white PE kits to say, 'I like you, we're gonna be friends.' I could do little to say no to such a request, and I admired her confidence. We quickly became inseparable. Evidently, I'm attracted to dominant personalities. After discovering that we lived in the same area, a mere walking distance from one another, we began doing the after-school journey home together and spent our Saturday afternoons at St George's Shopping Centre. This was all music to my mother's ears, as she previously worried that I'd be mugged on the bus ride home – and she wasn't *totally* wrong.

Attending a predominantly Asian school, there were only a handful of black kids in my year, and fewer who actually liked me.

Kizzle became my confidante, my high-school best friend, who kept the girls in the year above me at bay and threatened anyone who tried to bully me for no reason by giving them a stern 'don't even try it' look. She was my safety net, and I felt protected in her presence. After all, I weighed about the same as three pebbles, and people often joked that the wind could snap me. (They weren't entirely wrong.) Our whirlwind friendship meant lunchtimes spent learning the choreography to Cameo's 'Candy' and belting out the last note of JoJo's 'Too Little, Too Late' with precision. I felt comfortable.

But the fairy-tale friendship soon came to a halt when Kiz fell pregnant and it was my job to keep the secret under wraps. A good secret-keeper for my friends, I hid her pregnancy developments in the same way that characters do in TV shows when they're pretending they're not knocked up in real life. But when the news eventually broke school-wide, her maternity leave meant that I had no one to spend lunches with and that my references to the latest episode of *Half & Half* on Trouble would go unnoticed from there on out.

Her absence from school was felt *h e a v i l y*, as I went from being protected to being vulnerable and was now a direct target for the girls in the year above me. Kiz's absence from school left me exposed to the bullies she'd kept at bay, and they took it as a personal challenge to berate me on a daily basis. What started out as a shove here and there quickly turned into being pushed into walls and told that I was a 'dirty slag' on a regular basis. At one point, the intimate details of a private life that had yet to play out were proudly displayed on one of my bullies' Myspace profiles:

•?((¯°·._.• g€ţ 2 Ќɲ⊙ •._.·°¯))?•

LaUreN iS a SlAg

SH3 GETZ FUKKED IN CARZ

-DiiRTY BiiTCH

••?((¯°·._.• *dyn Kn☉ẃ* •._.·°¯))?•

A much bigger deal back then, it was the first time I'd been name-called like that – and with no cause. That bio stayed up for at least three months, and it sent pins through my body any time I read it. I had been labelled by a group of girls because I, an inexperienced teen, didn't engage in the same coital activities they did during lunch breaks and behind the hall stage. My reluctance to engage in amorous activities with one of the gross boys at school meant that not only was I called frigid by the boys, but labelled a slut by the girls. A word that people knowingly understood would cause more harm than good to a teen's reputation.

The incident that caused the minor bullying to turn into full-blown physical attacks was the day the new girl's tale was revealed on the schoolyard. She had gotten *intimate* with one of the three hot guys at school and had told my best friend, Kiz, via text, and then me IRL as to her I was cool by association. News spread throughout the school by lunchtime, and before I knew it, I was being confronted by a group of girls for being a 'snitch'. With no real idea of what was going on, I racked my brain about the potential secrets I might've spilled and came up blank.

'Watch,' said the new girl, who stood at five foot one, as she stared at me venomously, looking up at my five-foot-seven frame. 'We're gonna fuck you up!' I had never been in a fight – other than the sibling beatings I took from my brother for not letting him borrow my iPod Shuffle. I had zero interest in fighting, because one punch would have been enough to break me in two. So there I stood, numb. It only took ten minutes before she came back with a group of ten girls. She screamed a number of slurs about my (lack of) sexual encounters and my being a snitch. She eventually let on

34

that she believed me to be the person who had breached security and revealed that she had had coitus behind the school stage, but I was still so baffled by the whole interaction. 'I didn't tell anyone, what the hell?' I shakily said, before being told to shut up by one of the other ten girls. It was later revealed that the *boy* was the loose-lipped culprit, but the target on my forehead was already set and I had to prepare for battle. After school I saw a group of *more* girls waiting to beat me to a pulp at the gates, and I just knew my fate. My body collapsed in on itself as I panicked about how I would explain a bloodied, swollen face to my mother.

Luckily it wasn't to be, as I was snuck out the school's side exit by an old friend and managed to make a run for home without raising any alarms. However, this one escape was very much like *Final Destination*, as the beatings and the bullying would soon catch up with me. It was written.

The bullying became so severe that Year 10 was likely the least enjoyable year of my life – adult breakups excluded. I was followed home on multiple occasions, had my hair ripped out and tossed to the ground, got punched in the face and almost knocked out. It was . . . a lot. Eventually I stopped going to school altogether, and on the off chance that I did go in, I arrived late and left early. But I was too embarrassed to explain why I was so down, and instead dissociated from the situation entirely. Staying behind in lessons until the second alarm rang, I avoided the school corridor like the plague, as it was frequently the scene of my own personal hell.

I mean – look, in a way I get it. I was already considered a pretty weird kid as I was well versed in ripping and 'restyling' thrifted clothes, and my choice in music alone was enough to have me thrown into brick walls, but I still don't understand the lesson they were attempting to teach me. Perhaps my five-foot-one arch-enemy was just the catalyst my bullies needed for their tirades against me. After all, they were already keen to start on me for cocking my ponytail to the side and turning the volume down slightly when it reached the Slipknot songs on shuffle.

SEXLESS IN THE CITY

Ever fearful of having sex, the beginning of my teen years was scarred by stories of girls who could 'feel it in their stomachs' at a very young age. *It* being a penis. I only heard sordid sex stories via my promiscuous school companions, and on TV shows that offered a before-the-watershed PG version in comparison to my peers.

It was via my Sony Ericsson and the iconic online novel *Keisha Da Sket* that I learned what it meant to grind up on your crush and that foreplay could be accompanied by foreign objects. (Yes, I'm talking about *that* scene.) Up until then, I had only been told that my virginity needed to be saved for someone special, when I was really and truly ready. Spoiler alert: I don't think anyone is ever truly ready to smoosh genitals with someone for the first time. *Keisha Da Sket* was the titillating fanfiction you wish you had written but were entirely too embarrassed to admit you fantasised about. Despite being a virgin, late-night reruns of *Sexcetera* and feature-length soft porn flicks with a real storyline and minimal sex meant that you knew what sex was but had no desire to actually do it IRL. At thirteen and conflicted about my baser urges, I looked to the story of *Keisha Da Sket* as a release from my inner inhibitions. It was incredibly endearing to read the things you randomly thought about via a relatable story – and using early-2000s text slang no less. All the while being ignored by the first love of my life (shout out Adam).

A time that is now being memorialised in the TikTok era, just as we did with the 80s and 90s, the early 2000s was the blueprint and birthed the creatives manning the industry in the present day. Despite the rampant slut-shaming, *Keisha Da Sket* – clearly written from a woman's perspective – was the key to some of us being able to finally open up about one day 'giving it up' (word to Rihanna) to the next love of our life. Integral to the way we discuss sex in the present day, the story, which was sent via Bluetooth and infrared, helped to destigmatise the discussion of sex for girls. Albeit slightly.

Growing up, I can admit to being terrified of being vocal about being a virgin, losing my virginity and having wild thoughts when alone. UK hits like Dizzee Rascal's 'I Luv U', while catchy, only helped to add to the stigmatisation of women who were promiscuous – and if you're anything like me, kept you from bussing it like a dancehall singer for far too long in your adult years. Detrimental lyrics detailed how she was attractive, but after engaging in a six-way, could not be taken seriously. Young girls were told through songs that promiscuity was punishable by lifelong singleness and undesirability.

While a distinctive UK hit, 'I Luv U' in particular heavily contributed to how I felt about putting my mouth on a penis, until I was eighteen. Up until then – and my first real boyfriend – I was convinced that giving head meant giving way to promiscuity as a whole, and never being taken seriously as someone's future whatever. To paraphrase Charlotte York, I didn't want to become the 'in the mouth' girl. Hilarious, considering I've little desire to wed, but I digress. Dizzee's hit song left me questioning how I might be perceived by prospective partners had I ever given in to oral sex. At high school, labels like 'headerz' and 'headmout' were used as thinly veiled insults to discredit girls, and so these terms echoed in my head any time the desire washed over me. I refused to be one of *those* girls, despite eventually becoming one – a *Superhead*,[2] in fact.

In an opinion that is almost laughable in the present day, we were told that threesomes, foursomes and giving head were acts that

---

2   Karrine Steffans: iconic vixen, and well ahead of her time.

made you 'unwifeable' – all the while giving power to the opposite sex as they explored bumping nether regions with multiple partners. There was a heinous battle between being a freak bitch and a virginal future wife, but I believe men had no real idea what they wanted, and instead used these conflicting factors to rate women until they did.

The effects of the virginity complex mean women feel tremendous guilt for giving in when finally 'allowed' to. The obsession with being regarded as virginal, while also learning how to do everything required of a 'freak in the sheets', leaves us not knowing what to do at all. The language surrounding virginity has never sat right with me. From phrases like someone 'taking' your virginity or you 'losing' your V-card, the emphasis on it being a virtue stolen from a person has always made me quite uncomfortable. Once a woman has 'lost' her virginity, she enters into the unknown, trying desperately to restore a respect given only to those who have chosen to keep their virtue intact.

I greatly remember girls being too scared to admit that they had in fact deactivated their V-card, because it meant they might lose some semblance of respect from their peers – and in particular, prospective partners. In my case, I was told by someone I thought I teen-loved that I should have saved it for him. It's laughable looking back, but those words cut so deep at that time that I punished myself for finding a partner and trusting him enough to go the distance. Perhaps I should have waited.

I remember being asked the question 'Are you a virgin?' for the first time. Unsure of what this meant – but privy to lickadickaday pranks – I immediately answered 'NOoOoOo!' Subjected to ridicule in an attempt to *avoid* ridicule, I would later learn what it meant to be a virgin and protest the notion of *not* being a virgin, on the grounds that I didn't actually know what this term meant – before watching this prank be played out on every other unsuspecting young girl on the schoolyard. Early on, even before our knowledge of virginity and its proximity to 'purity', we were plagued with dangerous questions surrounding it.

Movies like *The 40-Year-Old Virgin* placed a lot of emphasis on the stark difference between men and women in terms of the virginity complex. While young women were taught that, by 'losing' their virginity, they were giving way to impurity and losing something from themselves, young men were taught that by not losing their virginity, they were emasculated or effeminate. In films like this one starring Steve Carell, we got a behind-the-scenes look at boys' locker room discussions. We saw that men were poked and prodded for waiting for the right moment – and the right person to share the experience with – and such conversations, while comedic, struck a chord.

Many of the ways in which we navigate intimate relationships follow preoccupations with control and owning women's sexuality. A social construct that benefits no one, this further aids the idea that you're losing something by giving in to urges. Deep-diving into this theory, I discovered that some parents regularly take their daughters to the gynaecologist to check that her hymen is still intact as a means of 'virginity testing'.

I've read on countless occasions that men view women differently after having a daughter of their own, but then they use an obsession with protecting virginity to fuel their agenda. From a very young age we're seen as objects to be protected, until we're later viewed as objects of desire.

With a number of 'wifey riddims' on the scene, teens began to question their desirability if they dared to step outside of the allocated body count. Should we dare to uphold the virginity complex and not give in to baser urges, we were at risk of being labelled 'frigid', a particularly unattractive quality to boys at that time. However, should you give in and let young men fulfil their three minutes of passion, you were a 'whore'. Looking back, is it any wonder literary txt books like *Keisha Da Sket* were the holy grail for those of us who wanted to try sex but had opted out for fear of the dreaded labels attached to it?

At school during the *Keisha Da Sket* era, while we were all engrossed in the same story, boys still used this as a means to slut-shame. The UK literary masterpiece was a gateway to a girl admitting that she *kind of* wanted to try sex out at some point. Despite late-night unsupervised viewings of *Sexcetera*, our understanding of sex was incredibly basic, with the few references discovered via fanfiction and tales from our classmates.

Understood only as 'private square tingles', with no grasp on what to do with this new-found horniness – and combined with an overwhelming desire to be touched while simultaneously being terrified of being touched – we were aimlessly leading one another. Recalling the difficulty of navigating teenage horniness and the rampant slut-shaming, I wish shows like *Big Mouth* had existed to let me know it was completely normal to desire things I had no real knowledge of. Much like Missy in *Big Mouth*, I longed to dry-hump through my Evisu jeans and worry about the outcome and subsequent mess later. Alas, the negative connotations only caused me to stray further away from wanting to engage at full capacity, and so hand strokes while sweatily holding hands at the cinema was the extent of my sexual experience at that time.

THE SLUT EFFECT

Growing up in an era that favoured pages exposing and outing promiscuous young teens, there was something very damaging about consuming this very specific type of content. Plagued by the knowledge that someday it could be your name mentioned in one of these accounts, detailing the men you may or may not have slept with, you lived in fear that it could be you next – without you ever having sampled the peen. Extensive in their research of your perfectly edited images – but not so much in the substance of their claims – 'slagsXposed' accounts read like the pages of unfiltered gossip magazines. Altered slightly for the new-age internet, these harmful lists separated girls from one another based on a new class status: slaggery. Even if you hadn't yet lost your virginity, you could be submitted to one of these pages by someone who hated you, detailing a body count you weren't even aware you had (because you didn't). One after the other, pages called things like 'slagsinNW', '[insertuniversity]exposed' and 'dailyexposed' would appear, follow your account and post relentless untruths about people you were in close proximity to.

Spending most of my life on the internet, I recently came across a video that expressed the change in the way we view sluttery today. With the slogan 'Hot Girl Summer' determining how we conduct ourselves once the sun is out, it's almost ironic that we're now being praised for embracing sluttery, when it was condemned only a few years prior. Putting women at the forefront of a sex-positive movement when we were once shamed for even thinking about sex is the power shift I always dreamt of. With women artists leading the charge and events like the SlutWalk made more prominent by celebrities such as activist and socialite Amber Rose, now more than ever it's okay to be promiscuous.

Having used Karley Sciortino's memoir *Slutever: Dispatches from an Autonomous Woman in a Post-Shame World* as a guide to exploring my sexuality, over time I've lessened the guilt I placed on myself for giving in to my baser urges. While in my youth I may have felt tremendous guilt for allowing my boyfriend to finger me for the first time, the adult version of me is simply glad I tried it at a young age so I know how to guide new partners in the present day.

Promiscuity or proximity to sex in any form was often condemned, shaming young girls out of even lipsing in hidden crevices of the schoolyard. Now we have whole anthems dedicated to freely enjoying our desires, and we can be the Promiscuous Girl of our own stories. Had I been born in a century that favoured sexual pleasure over the worry of contracting syphilis, perhaps I'd have died of that before being shamed for shagging it up.

Holly Valance's smash hit 'Kiss' was the proactive energy we were in awe of as kids and now embody as adults. Watching the well-lit video, we questioned whether she was really naked beneath the lights, and not only admired her confidence in being starkers but envied her for putting it out there in a music video. Think pieces about the singer being in the buff would dominate the media, but this video was one of the first times I understood that a woman's body is her own to do with as she pleases (while media portrayals continued to inform us that it wasn't our choice at all). Seeing how society shamed women who bared all while simultaneously placing emphasis on the greased-up topless models on Page 3, we understood that a feminine body existed only to appease the male gaze and that it was maddening if she chose to expose herself for herself.

Once upon a time, the declaration of self-love found in the ample grainy bikini selfies we share online would have been deemed abhorrent and whorish. Self-love shots on Instagram used to be seen as evidence of a lack of self-respect and that we were unworthy of the title 'future wifey'. We need to give thanks to the rappers who paved the way for us – Lil' Kim, Foxy Brown, Missy Elliott, Nicki Minaj and Megan Thee Stallion, to name a few – and helped to destigmatise women's sexuality. Detailing their preferences in how to get it in, tracks like 'One Minute Man' expressed how to prioritise a woman's preferences in the sexual encounters that previously only favoured the male orgasm.

On the other side, catchy songs like Destiny's Child rhythmic 'Nasty Girl' upheld the ideals that women had to dress a certain way in order to be deemed worthy of respect. Artistically a bop, but lyrically detrimental to those of us who wished to bare our midriffs and thighs entirely while caring not for the male gaze, songs like this one would be damaging to people who felt they'd lose the respect of their peers for simply bussing it open that one time. Slut-shamed via a catchy R&B track, we sang the lyrics at the top of our lungs and without a second thought, not realising how harmful its lyrical content could be to our self-worth. Subconsciously trained to cover up so as to appease men and later gain a husband, the words echoed in our heads as we pressed Decline on the sexual decisions our coochies screamed 'YES PLEASE' to.

Early 2000s hits heavily contributed to the idea that women had to follow a specific set of rules in order to be deemed worthy of respect. Paramore's catchy lyrics in 'Misery Business', which label a girl a whore as the video depicts a woman being slut-shamed, feel out of step today. We've since had to detach from and rid ourselves of the stigmas that plagued us in our formative years, as songs like this one were instrumental in making us feel terrible about our life choices post-haste. Slut-shaming anthems topped the charts, and Christina Aguilera's feminist anthem 'Can't Hold Us Down' – and the video's close-up shots of the side slits of her purple shorts that dominate my nostalgic Pinterest boards – was just the hit we needed to shake things up and break the mould. Though it was just a catchy tune for many, with few taking in its lyrical content, the banger referred to the gross double standards between men and women when it came to sexuality. Detailing the ways in which women were scolded for expressing sexual tendencies, the hit released in 2002 is still a homerun today.

Addressing the notion of falsifying rumours in order to ruin a woman's reputation and slandering one's name, this track is right up there as one of my favourite women's empowerment songs. At the ripe old age of sixteen, being called a 'total slag' (as self-proclaimed by Kat Slater) was the ultimate diss. Unable to shake these stigmas once they'd been attached to your full name and online profile, the tarnishing title meant that you were painted with the *Scarlet Letter* 'A'. Friends were actively told they shouldn't hang with you, because your 'reputation' might ruin their reputation and thus their polished virginal brand. I am inadvertently telling my own story here.

> *Growing up in the UK, there were a number of titles that could either make or break you as a young woman (or man, I guess). There was nothing more damaging or terrifying than being branded a 'headmout*[3] *or 'bocat',*[4] *because for some inane reason we believed that if you dared to put genitalia in your mouth you would be cursed with mouth ulcers, dry lips and whatever else. Once titled you were unkissable, un-talk-to-able and lacking in basic human decency.*

> —Lauren Rae, *one of five thousand newsletters*

Grossly misinformed about our twenties and thirties being the 'fun years', we were led to believe that we could have sexy-time fun without consequence. Well, other than STIs and, in some cases, unplanned pregnancies. Before settling down and starting a family – if you so choose – we're told nowadays via various channels that we're more than welcome to buss it open and split in di middle for those we find attractive, but even during my 'hoe phase' I felt a sense of shame after the fact with each brief encounter. Ever uncomfortable with fully exploring my sexuality – due to the harsh

---

3   *Headmout* – to go down on a man
4   *Bocat* – to go down on a woman

terms heard in my younger years – the fear of shaming and back-lash kept me from ever becoming an Abella Danger[5] behind closed doors. The labels of 'whore', 'slut' and 'hedonist', even before I'd engaged in amorous activities, scared me entirely out of swinging from the shower rod like Mimi Faust.

With such conflicting conversations surrounding sexual experiences, is it any wonder we were shamed out of safely and con-sentingly enjoying sex?

Now a self-proclaimed whore, I granted myself this title after being nudged for being even a little promiscuous in my twenties and teens. To the men I found attractive this wasn't the fun ploy I thought it would be, as I was later given the title of 'local bike'. Lessening my self-worth and the way I viewed myself, these small comments and the bullying that surrounded them affected the way I carried myself – and that's true even to this day. Flitting some-where between 'I don't give a fuck' and 'I wonder what they'll think of me', my poor decision-making – particularly in my choice of men – led me to believe I was worth less each time I had a sexual encounter, be it big or small. To paraphrase Keyshia Cole in her hit 'I Should Have Cheated', I should have just slutted it out.

---

5   Google at your own risk, preferably on incognito mode in your web browser

The Writer on Wine, Booze, and Everything In Between

Chapter 2: The Writer On Wine, Booze & Everything In Between

To paraphrase Judy Blume, 'Are you there, God? It's me, the frequent drinker.'

Although I maintain that problems with alcohol are not a joke, I can't help but think that my introduction to drinking was. Surely my parents knew I'd fall into a hapless routine of booze > hangover > rest in bed all day > repeat, or else they would've stopped my drinking dead at the age of fourteen when I first got drunk.

I don't have many people to blame for my slight reliance on alcohol, but I believe the women in my life helped determine my fate. I'm often told the story of my granny rubbing rum into my gums when I was a baby, to ease the pain of teething and also to put me to sleep. So, looking back, my first drunk experience probably happened a lot earlier than I can recall. But I'm entirely thankful. If not for having rum rubbed on my gums, I might have suffered at Oceana in my teens. Instead, I watched everyone else vomit outside the venue and all over their New Look dresses – or worse, pass out and shit themselves at university. I was put in the training camp of drinking from early on and taught the dos and don'ts.

I know where it began and when 'I'll just have a glass' turned into 'Christ almighty, I need a bottle'. As a child, my best friend and I would watch in awe as our mothers tapped their cigarette ash into fancy mosaic ashtrays, sipped Merlot and gossiped about adult life. We wanted to be just as fabulous when we were older, so the natural order of things was to follow suit and pick up a habit that looked sophisticated as fuck, i.e. drinking.

Soon enough, we were purchasing bottles of our own and eventually discussing our own adult problems, with topics ranging from 'I fear my boyfriend doesn't love me anymore' to 'We've got the keys, we're homeowners'. In a flash, we'd become our mothers, and were sitting at dining tables dishing on life's little (or large) problems. Officially 'adulting' in our eyes, we were emulating the women we adored the most. Little by little it became almost disrespectful to turn up to anyone's home without a bottle of red, and arriving empty-handed would almost certainly warrant a trip to the local offy to get a bottle of Prosecco for no particular fucking reason. Before we knew it, we were rewarding ourselves with a glass (or five) at the end of each day for simply making it through a hard day's work. Wine became a cause for celebration. We were celebrating life, love (or the lack thereof) and booze.

Over the years I've come to realise that alcohol is where I exercise the most self-control. Though I may not *always* be able to distance myself from friends who might not have my best interest at heart and the romantic encounters I'm well aware are wrong for me, I *do* know when to stop necking bevvies and how much to sip after a seemingly long day at work. My experiences with wine are vastly different to those of other people, as booze has become part of my overall brand. While alcohol was maybe forbidden to adolescents in most households growing up, and perhaps, as a result, many of those individuals frequently ended up face down in their own vomit on a night out, my own experience was quite the opposite. Instead I left behind all those embarrassing scenarios when I learned my limits at seventeen in a rather unfortunate treehouse vomit incident.

Although it seemed all glitz and glamour, the reality was that our introduction to alcohol was, of course, fuelled by lies, trickery and deceit – manipulative skills I no longer possess, unfortunately. Growing up, one of my best friends and I were heralded as the 'responsible' preteens. This meant we were often awarded adult privileges that usually involved handling and distributing booze. In what I can only imagine was payback for my mother's eight hours in labour, we were cast in the roles of busboy and bartender at family get-togethers. Distributing alcohol to all the adults, my best friend and I would gracefully refill and collect glasses with a smile. We took our roles very seriously, but we also knew that half a glass of Prosecco each as payment just wasn't enough for us mini drinkers in the making. We had a taste for alcohol and only wanted more, and evidently this is something that has stayed with me through to adulthood, as it would later see me collecting an abundance of Spider-Man memorabilia and getting an array of small tattoos just because. Playing bartender for the evening meant that we could drink in secret without our mothers knowing, as we refilled the adults' glasses (sorry Mum).

Evenly pouring Prosecco into each glass, we crafty adolescents made sure we could get at least one full glass to share between the two of us out of each bottle. It's a wonder I wasn't recruited into a cartel of some sort. The thrill, theatrics and early-onset tipsiness made the whole operation incredibly entertaining. It was forbidden . . . kinda? Even as I type this, I understand why Eve did what she had to do with that apple.

That introduction to drinking saw two preteens develop a taste that would ruin their bank accounts later on in life. Had we sipped cans of Coke instead, we'd only be subject to rotting teeth and cavities, and not a penchant for alcohol.

I'LL HAVE YOU KNOW, WINE *IS* A PERSONALITY TRAIT

I take it as a personal challenge to refute the notion that pizza and wine cannot be referred to as personality traits. Because I hope that when people see me, they immediately think of red wine, associating it with part of the full Lauren package – and not to be seen as a negative thing. It's similar to Penny Hofstadter's affiliation with Sauvignon Blanc in *The Big Bang Theory*, and wine mums who say quirky things like 'it's five o'clock somewhere'. To me, the true mark of wine being a personality trait when describing yourself to new people is that it's an activity enjoyed without self-judgement.

It might be mentioning alcohol in a dating profile or making comments to friends that suggest you're made up of 99 per cent of whatever your favourite drink is, but I'll hold my hands up and say wine is one of the things I list when people ask what my hobbies include. And given that my only real hobbies include wine, Netflix and curating Spotify playlists – really, this is my entire personality.

Before experiencing 18+ club culture in full, I was introduced to clubbing via under-18 raves. These teen-specific events meant that I could practise my Usher and Beyoncé club-entry walks to the very best of my ability while channelling true main-character energy, just perhaps reimagined in brightly coloured clothing paired with flat dolly shoes. Covering all bases, each event promised one cola per person, and its main ingredient – caffeine – saw me dance the night away to the likes of Soulja Boy and Lil Jon & The East Side Boyz, with dance routines I'd got down to a tee prior to entering the club.

Integrating us into a world that would soon become the norm from eighteen until twenty-something, U18 raves were the perfect introduction to evenings of vivrant gyrating and sweaty brows, resulting in curled hair by the end of the night. Promptly ending at 11 p.m., these events (which, when you were spotted by your peers, were the ticket to a climb in social status) helped to form a relationship with the latest trends in music, style and social interactions, particularly with members of the opposite sex. Of course, one cola per person later transformed into shots of apple Sourz and vodka mixers at the bar in Oceana. A daring new fascination with mixed drinks, mortifying falls in front of the bouncer and breaking Primark heels on impact meant that Facebook albums entitled 'Last SatURday' encapsulated what it meant to forge a personality from alcohol.

Adopting routines that involved pre-drinks, shots at the chosen destination and then relying on whatever stranger fancied us the most to fund the rest of the evening, the transformation in me that happened with alcohol was not unlike the Hulk's. Completely changing from mild-mannered to the girl who was up for anything – often dancing on tables and snogging hot, age-appropriate strangers – alcohol became my central personality, as I adored the commentary about how different sober Lauren was to drunk Lauren.

Despite the internet regularly informing us that habits like eating pizza and guzzling wine by the gallon are unequivocally *not* personality traits, I stand tall in disagreeing. Unlike the wine mums of our office lives – who preface every Monday-morning meeting with a brief play-by-play of a booze-filled weekend – I have substance behind these claims.

I spend a small portion of each day researching the questions I'm too embarrassed to bother my friends with, and Reddit has quickly become my safe haven for this very reason. A hub to find answers to the stupidest questions that plague my mind – from my intrigue about sex lives in the 1800s to ridiculous conspiracy theories I believe to be true – Reddit has become the driving force for my assertion that alcohol can be a personality trait. After scouring subreddit threads to support my claim, the gist of my findings was that most people bothered by the notion of claiming it as a trait were mostly just irritated by the parading of empty glasses on social media profiles, as opposed to the actual act of drinking. These people seemed to be bothered entirely by the raucous clinking of glasses and the faces that read 'we've clearly had one too many'.

While many disgruntled Reddit users were miffed about Instagram users using the consumption of alcohol to seem more interesting and outgoing, I was curious. Were these individuals simply annoyed at having never been invited to house parties where teens snuck in alcopops and consumed shots of Disaronno when mildly peer-pressured? Perhaps they deplored drinking as a whole, never having experienced the hilarity of post-drinking stories or the beauty of a well-priced bottomless brunch.

Looking deeper into the 'myth' of drinking as a personality trait, I noticed that people were triggered by the fact that it was a self-proclamation. Much like those who are rattled by confident people, the upset was that these people were showboating or gloating that they were able to hold their liquor without flailing – or at least this is what I assumed. I came to understand that people claiming that alcohol is a personality trait bothers people more than the act of drinking itself.

I engaged in drinking from a young age, at a time where legally I wasn't supposed to and in settings that would likely be deemed crime scenes today. At that time, being sixteen and swigging Glen's Vodka directly from the bottle *was* a personality trait, as it determined whether or not you were cool enough to hang with the kids who climbed fences and set up camp in school fields after-hours. With crumpled blazers, two £4 bottles of vodka between ten people, and a group of kids who knew not how to handle alcohol nor its after-effects, this very specific and typically British entryway to drinking spirits is what separated the brave from the not-so-brave. We were living out our live-action *Skins* fantasy at the most basic level – with the only vodkas our local off-licence allowed us to purchase.

Although the UK TV series *Skins* delved into hard-hitting issues like eating disorders and the mental-health conditions among teens that likely contributed to some of our problems today, our primary focus when watching it was elsewhere – lost in the allure of rebelling with friends and getting, as they frequently referred to it as, 'monumentally fucked up'. The drama series followed the tumultuous lives of a group of teenagers in Bristol. These early-2000s grunge kids dressed provocatively in rebellious teen couture – and Effy Stonem's combination of smudged eyeliner and mysterious constantly hungover state especially – would be one of many references I came to know in the glow-up of my wine personality trait later in life.

The onscreen rampant sweaty parties fuelled by drinking from the bottle and stumbling out of establishments uncontrollably drunk had an allure to them – one we could relate to, as we weren't yet old enough to party anywhere other than the local pub. And while our only experience of drinking came to us courtesy of not yet knowing when to stop – resulting in alcohol poisoning lite – the relatability factor of this hit series meant that we saw ourselves in their kick-backs and after-college house parties.

Decked out in our finest Lonsdale and Lyle & Scott attire – similarly to our *Skins* counterparts – we wreaked havoc on our crushes via drunk texting, and purposely pressed all of the keys to convey that we were pissed. Later, our love of at-the-weekend bevvies and after-work pints grew into it being the only thing we could base a conversation on around new people. We prefaced every story with 'well, I was pretty fucked up', and excused our bad decisions with 'in all fairness, I *was* pissed'. Poor decision-making when under the influence became the perfect excuse and the best way to distance ourselves from bad situations.

Tumblr had a chokehold on our overall aesthetic of looking rough after a night out, and we tried to convey that, while we maybe shouldn't have been, we were indeed cool enough to drink alcohol. Such outside influences heavily contributed to how we shaped ourselves in regards to drinking as a personality trait. Posing with a Strongbow lager in our Primark hoodies, these pivotal Facebook memories helped rate us in terms of the cool factor.

Merely flies on the wall of our own terrible decision-making, consumption of alcohol in our formative years helped to curate more interesting tales in nights out to come. Embarrassing oneself with the intent that it might someday make a great drunken story was the driving force behind a large number of these poor decisions.

Wine as a personality trait does not start and end with being able to tell the difference between Cabernet Sauvignon from Malbec. Being able to steer a conversation directly to drunken escapades in an interaction that does not call for it is an art form. Via my extensive research I've found that many non-drinkers have adopted the theory that those who frequent alcohol do so to appear more leisurely, to further distance themselves from those who drink simply because they enjoy it. The mere thought of raucously clinking glasses is too much to bear for some, reminded of the incessant Prosecco-flute Boomerangs posted by mums about town on Instagram.

Those quaint signs that read 'Home is where the Prosecco is', 'It's Prosecco o'clock somewhere' and 'Prosecco made me do it' might be daunting to the untrained eye. Personally, I think that homeware stores need to be held accountable for the number of written signs available to the public, and I will remind myself of this if ever I place a rhyming quote above the toilet in the en suite of my future residence.

Add to this the plethora of Prosecco-themed workouts, and it's clear the ridiculousness of Prosecco propaganda has absolutely gotten out of hand – this I can admit to. Though I say this with love, of course. Studies show that Prosecco sales broke records in 2019, likely due to the influx of bottomless brunch spots capitalising off of those of us who enjoy having a beverage on the cheap. But decorating the inside of our homes with this message is out of the question. In a nightmare of my own, I envision wall-to-wall hangings with terrible puns in every room of the house.

Growing up, the BBC played host to a number of my favourite TV shows, all of which had me in a veritable chokehold from 7.30 p.m. onwards. I elicited a lot of my personality from my onscreen besties Edina Monsoon and Patsy Stone from *Absolutely Fabulous* – decked out as they were in Christian Lacroix's most vibrant printed pieces and sleek all-leather looks. I'd always dreamed of being a rich singleton, terrified of getting serious with men but in possession of a fully stocked Champagne fridge, a best friend who refused to leave my side and an onslaught of drunken escapades. Not a far cry from my current lifestyle, the hit TV series was integral in defining what it meant not to give a fuck about getting trashed with your best mate. And in high fashion, no less.

Screaming that she'd only had a single bloody drink while concealing her three-bottle-minimum hangover, Eddy's line in the show's pilot episode in 1992 spoke volumes to me, and it came to be how I prefaced any interaction where I sensed judgement towards my drinking habits. With guilt taking centre stage, my ability to tell the truth about what *really* took place the night before is a rarity. Particularly around people who ask the questions re: the night before with judgemental overtones. Unfazed by their week-long binges, Edina and Patsy helped to destigmatise women drinking excessively – at least for me.

In the narrative that sees women who drink as sloppy, getting drunk is often followed by the image of falling into a bush post-bottomless brunch. The early 2000s saw celebrities, viewed as hedonists who sought instant gratification, falling out of the butt end of cabs knees first. Wanting to be as far as possible from this portrayal of drunkenness, you always feared becoming one of the pappz'd babes questioning their life choices in the back of an extortionately priced black cab after a night out at one of Mayfair's finest clubs. Showing these women with their heads bowed in shame against the onslaught of unsolicited flash photography, these images were burned into our brains. As was the street scene taken in Manchester on New Year's Day that went viral in 2016. Like a modern Renaissance painting, this iconic photo represents how drinkers are viewed by non-drinkers.

With upskirting shots at the forefront of paparazzi celebrity photos, the media in the early 2000s was heavily dominated by callous propaganda that saw alcohol as the enemy. Sprawled across the pages of red-top newspapers, women were portrayed as undignified when seen to be having fun and suspected of being unable to handle their drink for simply being drunk when they were snapped without consent. Etched into my memory are a series of brightly flashed photos of celebrities stumbling around the streets of London in stylish mini-dresses. Concealing their dignity with one hand while the other shoos away a photographer, these images deterred us from living out our best drunken lives for fear of judgement from Facebook friends at a later date.

Having partied since the ripe old age of fourteen, I've experienced the progression of one free plastic cup of Coca-Cola with my Dreamz ticket to Sambuca shots priced at £1.50. With this levelling up came a barrage of new experiences during parties. Learning the boundaries of how provocatively to dress, whining our waists to Vybz Kartel's latest hit, and ungracefully plonking ourselves into overpriced group taxis, we soon learned what was deemed as worthy of respect versus what was seen as sloppy by onlookers.

While it was easier to get drunk at this age with your closest group of friends, there was always the worry that you might be the friend who needed to be sent home in a cab early – or worse yet, the friend that passed out in the middle of a great night out. There was always one, and you just hoped it was never you. Toeing the line between merry and blackout drunk, there was an art to being the fun-loving drinker who never turned down a round but also opting out as soon as the sights around you began to blur. Wearing our most provocative ensembles to ensure entry into clubs as freshly turned eighteen-year-olds, we used the myth that the alcohol we were downing by the gallon would warm our bodies to explain the truly terrible combination of short bodycon skirts, cropped tops and wedge heels we wore in the winter rain. And this continued after our switch to a swanky university lifestyle – though I use the term 'swanky' lightly, as it was only one level higher than our college lives: the level called uni halls. We found beauty in truly catastrophic conditions and mould-infested premises, as our grotty first-year flats played host to the worst crime scenes you can imagine, where nights began with games of Ring of Fire and ended with at least one member of the gang passed out on the communal kitchen sofa.

The transition to university was smooth, but the evolution to drinking at university was even smoother. We no longer had to sneak in to our parents' homes after-hours or spend time aimlessly standing outside the kebab shop after the club had closed. This new-found freedom saw young adults wearing less and going out more, frolicking in new groups and inviting people back home just because they could. Making out with your crush on your doorstep wasn't the scandal it was when you lived with your parents, and we relished in the fact that our poor choices could only affect us, without fear of: 1) disturbing our parents and 2) the upstairs light switching on just as we turned the key in the front door. The overall experience of drinking at university was heightened by the thrill of not getting caught, and there not being any real consequences to our actions. With no one to answer to, the only thing we really had to worry about were the hangovers we were subjected to and the individuals we probably shouldn't have lipsed at Liquid last night.

Touring the university grounds upon arrival meant mapping how far your walk from the strip was to your flat. How many drunken steps it would take to make sure you were home in good time and free to urinate in the comfort of your own en-suite bathroom, so that you no longer needed to strip entirely naked in order to free yourself from the jumpsuit or playsuit you just *had* to wear on the drunkest night of the week. We understood that if we fell victim to wetting ourselves because we couldn't undo the clasp on our playsuit in time, at the very least we'd do it in our own home. I'd be lying if I said this hasn't happened to me.

Finally of legal age, buying alcohol at our local off-licence and Tesco became a riveting experience, as we could select whatever we wanted to craft deadly cocktails for one of the fifteen group events that week. Mixing a dangerous number of spirits to concoct a potion fit to wake the sleeping dead, vodka soon became a last resort as rum entered the chat and stole the entire fucking show. It showed us that we could indeed get monumentally fucked up without the burning sensation in our chest and a headache that screamed 'well, why the fuck did you think you could drink an *entire* bottle?' the next morning. Pre-drinks were just the beginning of our dedication to getting drunk enough to pose for photographers at raves, and we were more than happy to do so when under the influence. Pre-drinks at home also helped to see us through to the main event, and were a necessity for intoxication on a budget. Often better than the event itself, we'd gather a group of like-minded people and engage in games that should've been outlawed. (This is a direct reference to the dreaded 'dirty pint'.) Making sure to enter the club absolutely obliterated so as to make the most of the sweaty dance solos to come, we took umpteen shots to make sure our pre-drinks event was well worth it, so that we needn't spend any money at the venue and so that we wouldn't feel chilly in our rave-only outfits. Teens without a care, we carried our clear plastic cups with a swig of Coca-Cola and enough rum to power a small jet engine with pride.

However, with the carefree, fun-living drunken attitudes we adopted at university came an abundance of new labels ready to shame us out of having any real fun and to deter us from falling over in our miniskirts, laughing at our own sheer stupidity. Despite student union nights filled with scantily clad young men whipping out their uncensored willies for all to see, drinking excessively was seen as laddish, and when women did it we were harshly judged. It you dared exceed the limit and trip in your £14.99 New Look heels, you were a sloppy drunk who could *not* handle her booze, while the men of our age group decorated the streets with their vomit in shifts. When it came to those who passed out curled up by the toilet bowl at a house party, the rules favoured our male counterparts who also could not hold their liquor.

Just as women were called names for their sexual exploration, messy drinkers were routinely only called out if they were a woman. As I recall it, getting absolutely shitfaced at university was a trip – and a fantastic trip at that. We made out with strangers who went to the same university and claimed them as our boyfriends for the night. From the plastic cups of Sambuca shots to the umpteen beer chasers for our Jägerbombs, there was no real way to remain sober unless we stayed indoors. At £1 to £1.50 a shot, there was no greater high than that of a student night out. Stops at McDonald's were mandatory, calling for a Filet-O-Fish at the top of our lungs and never actually eating the meal, but instead falling asleep in it. Or better yet, beside it. These memories are precious, and though I've found slightly classier ways to be drunk when out, it's still as exciting as it ever was.

Many times over the years I've tried the completely sober thing, where all social drinking ceased and no after-work bottles of wine were consumed. Determined to move away from socialised drinking, I attempted to be responsible and drank smoothies in the morning and sparkling water all day instead. Until ultimately, I realised I was serving nobody by starving myself of the things I enjoy. This pause in alcohol consumption did nothing but prove I was stopping myself from drinking so as to appease those who were concerned, because they only knew of me screaming 'AYEEE' while holding a glass via my lengthy Instagram stories. Following the lead of some of my favourite onscreen drinkers, I came to understand that these kinds of decisions need not be made due to the judgement of others. Instead, they should be based on how I feel. I'm reminded again of *Ab Fab*, when Edina details the time Patsy attempted to quit drinking and lasted a mere eight hours.

At the risk of sounding clichéd, these dramatic onscreen portrayals of alcohol-infused adventures helped to shape my personality. I often reference Stoli-Bolli with prospective new friends, and make it a talking point with anyone I hope has seen the 90s show. Edina and Patsy's reluctance to be sober is something I aspire to. Patsy's love of booze underpinned her character too, and abstaining entirely would be a focal point throughout the series. Her resistance to giving up the bottle is something that I saw for myself in the future – to be ever accompanied by an expensive bottle of Champagne to complete my outfit and see me through my trips to Harvey Nichols.

In truth, Edina and Patsy's relationship with Bolli and Stoli was stronger than most connections found on Tinder and Bumble following a bored evening spent swiping right, just to keep your thumb busy. Their relationship with this concoction represented a deeper connection to me. Although, that connection often left them with truly terrible hangovers the following morning. Without realising it, I was channelling Edina and Patsy throughout my years at university, as my lack of care for consumption would lead me to some incredibly funny experiences later on.

YOU DRANK THIS – HERE'S WHY
YOU SHOULDN'T HAVE

With indulgence in alcohol comes an abundance of stupid decisions made while engaging in alcohol-fuelled activities. It's easy
to throw caution to the wind and send those drunken texts when
powered by an overwhelming desire to forget the trials and tribulations of life.

I'll let you in on a secret I'm sure everyone knows but most
choose not to acknowledge. We all know exactly what we're doing
when we're pissed. I knew exactly who I was going to drunkenly
and messily text hours before consuming alcohol, but blaming the
bottles I downed made for a less embarrassing story down the line.
Granted, we may not remember the *content* of what was confessed
while under the influence, but I must admit to having committed
these acts with intent. Even when heavily under the influence, I
must've wanted to do it – because I did it.

Drinking excessively but 'responsibly' tends to be my MO,
and I'm guided by the inappropriate texts that sober me refuses
to press Send on. Fuelled by the twerking little me who screams
'Tell him you fancy him!' to the tune of 'Big Ole Freak', my ability
to say no to myself when under the influence is slim to none. I'm
powerless to stop my own version of sharply dressed Buddy Love,
whose confidence calls all the shots. Chock-full of assurance about
my game, drunk-dialling is the driving force of the dumb decisions
sobriety prevents us from making.

Being single poses a number of challenges. For one thing, there
is no dedicated person to discuss the TV series you binge-watched
together, and for another you've no one to forcefully share new Spotify
finds with. But I think worst of all is not having a person to dial when
intoxicated. Having been single-single for quite some time now, I've

grown accustomed to drunk-texting my friends with a declaration of my love for them. Detailing my admiration, these text messages have no boundaries and are often lengthy and make little to no sense. But post-brunch feels call for more risqué texts, and in the moments when your independent singleness has hindered you in refreshing your contacts with new meat, ultimately there is a problem.

Watching your friends as they schedule dick appointments and cuddling sessions while you scroll through your recent call log for potential D only to think: *Mum, Mum . . . Friend I'm with currently . . . When TF did I call . . . Hi – oh ok, nvm.* Though I hate to admit it, I adore attention and adoration, purely so I can be repulsed by it, and this feeling is grossly intensified by the consumption of alcohol. I often find myself at a loss as to who to send blurry (but cute) selfies to, and end up calling other friends to complain while my drinking companions schedule their late-night rendezvous over FaceTime. A persistent lack of male attention means that contacts put in storage – only to be pulled out in truly catastrophic situations – are released for one more dopamine hit of rampant stupidity. Pulling out the 'long time' and 'it's been a minute' from my ass because the ample glasses of Prosecco have rid me of any shame entirely.

To this day, I find only two types of people who tell the whole truth: children and drunk people. And yes, I'm still holding on to the time my niece told me that I smelled after I'd travelled halfway across the country (Harrow to Essex) just to cuddle her. The reason is that children don't know what they're not supposed to say aloud just yet, and drunk people just cannot keep it in. I've lost count of the number of times I've tried to drunkenly call my friends at 3 a.m. to tell them of the time they wronged me in 2006, or about how I lied and don't really like their new dress from PLT. Luckily for me, they never answer, and are likely just now figuring out why they once had seventeen missed calls from Lauren at 3.39 a.m. on a Saturday morning. These are my confessions.

The human filter is a funny concept, and given that I already severely lack one, it's probable that 'alcohol x an overladen brain = drunk-texting anyone that I hope will reply' is a maths equation I should've learned in my university lectures. Drunken confessions remain my favourite thing in the world, second only to finding lost socks under the bed. There's absolutely nothing more thrilling than your drunk friend dramatically confessing something they've already told you once before. The theatrics of it are fantastic, and the setting, usually a bathroom, is where all secrets are released like they're tabloid news. Having heard many confessions over what was supposed to be casual drinks at the bar, I've grown fond of this kind of five-minute exchange.

Then there are those who confess deep, dark secrets, knowing neither of us will even remember having had the conversation – it's likely only to reappear in the form of a flashback you swear blind is a dream. This is also where I've admitted to the unthinkable, in the hopes that perhaps my friends will understand. I'm talking about the awkward first crushes on cartoon characters, confessing to 'accidentally' watching hentai that *one* time and/or openly admitting to never having watched Beyoncé's *Lemonade*. We all have sins, okay?

WHY DO WRITERS DRINK?

Someone once told me that they believed writers to be rather sullen people who spend their days drinking and essentially wasting their lives. Without realising it, this person read me for filth, because I can confirm that this is 100 per cent fact. Well, in my case it is.

A modern-day Carrie Bradshaw, despite the difference in drink of choice, I'm habitually pictured cuddled up next to a bottle of red. We're an ecosystem, red wine and I. I claim to drink in the name of creativity, but the truth is, drinking remains my favourite after-work activity, topic of conversation and Olympic sport. In fact, it's highly probable that I drink a little more often than I even realise sometimes. Carrie had her preferred selection of cigarettes and Cosmopolitans, and red wine is my own vice. Not only does it go down like breast milk does for a baby, it's also an aesthetic choice and more than *just a drink*. It adds to the contemporary TV character I see myself as.

Convincing myself that wine contains the right number of calories and offers unique health benefits helps to support the concept that my drinking alcohol after a hard day is justified. Almost as though it's a medical requirement. It's been said that the antioxidants in red wine aid a longer life span and are a preventative against inflammation and disease, which means realistically I should be immune to all illness as I'm quite certain that I am made of red wine by this point.

Unsurprisingly, I'm one of those *SATC* superfans who truly believes we were supposed to learn from Carrie, Samantha, Miranda and Charlotte. When it came time for Carrie to part ways with Marlboro Lights, I sympathised and understood first-hand the difficulties of unsubscribing yourself from something that has become your staple. Much like my adoration of the colour green and its appearance in 90 per cent of my Instagram feed, Carrie's packets of cigs were part of her overall aesthetic, and the same is true of myself with a glass of red.

In the hopes that I wasn't the only writer who frequented alcohol, I did a little digging and found that it's actually not just me. Terrified that I could potentially . . . maybe, be just a little bit on my own on this one, I was beyond ecstatic to discover that the fucking *Guardian* had come to my rescue. In 2013, Blake Morrison penned an entire article called 'Why Do Writers Drink?' and I couldn't have been happier. In fact, drinking, writing and being a drunk writer are totally and completely a thing. Not to steal the *entire* concept of the theatre production *Shit-faced Shakespeare*, but to me everything works better when there are no filters.

So as not to bore you with the statistics of it all, the article that saved me from re-evaluating my life choices suggests that writers drink more than other social groups – be that lawyers, doctors or shop assistants (although I spent many of my weekends working at House of Fraser absolutely trashed). But I digress. Kingsley Amis wrote in his book *Memoirs* that alcohol makes us less self-critical and allows us to write more fluidly. As someone who only knows how to go back, reread and self-criticise, I can tell you that's a fact. With more freedom in the words we craft – though we're likely talking out of our asses – we're able to write more fluidly, because it apparently reduces the fear.

Reduces fear. It fucking reduces fear. Though putting work out is equally as exciting as it is terrifying, I can't be the only writer whose body goes numb after publishing and then publicising a new piece. Will it be harshly critiqued? Will it be taken in the wrong context? Will it be sent out to a series of critical group chats to be dissected and disintegrated, as were my beloved superheroes in the *Avengers: Infinity War* epic?! Ultimately, although it's not the healthiest of coping mechanisms, I was using alcohol as a coping mechanism. It became a way to calm myself in a moment of sheer and utter panic about writing. The link between writing and drinking to ease the nerves exists in part because of an overactive impulse to self-criticise your work before it's even been published. Though with imposter syndrome holding so many of us by the throat, I'm often left wondering why we even give a toss who likes what we've put out into the stratosphere and who doesn't.

Someone once said, 'Write drunk, edit sober', which I've since found out is completely and utterly not a Hemingway quote. Thanks a lot, internet. The point is, it's a quote I live by in my day-to-day real life – 9-to-5.30 job excluded. When creating my own pieces (and yes, I'm likely a little tipsy while compiling this very book), I'm accompanied by a large glass of red wine. It sounds almost silly at this point, but wine helps to clear my mind of the lesser thoughts that plague me, and instead helps me to focus on the task at hand. In that moment, and after only one deserved sip, I am able to freely write all the F-bombs that have been clogging my brain, and decorate a Word document with colourful language that my granny might've told me I ought to 'wash my mouth out' for using. Whoever you are, person who *actually* invented this quote, I greatly commend you for providing me with a curated selection of words so dear to my heart. If not for the abundance of words already tattooed on my skin – and fear of never getting another job – I would more than likely have this penned in ink on my forehead.

YOU SURE YOU SHOULD DRINK THAT, HONEY?

When I look back on my tumultuous relationship with alcohol – namely vodka, Wray and his Nephew, and undisclosed amounts of rosé – I can't help but be thankful for its significant life lessons. Watching my friends drink white rum from the bottle taught me that perhaps not all of us are built with the demon spirit within. And what watching my granny drink vodka on the rocks taught me was that Caribbean women are built differently – they are special, even. Growing up in a typically Caribbean household where reggae music blasted on a Sunday morning and dinner was served promptly at 2 p.m. with a rum and coke, I'm indifferent to the snide remarks made by newcomers to my circle. It's cultural, and to be respected.

My life with alcohol has been a series of endless lols and life lessons, from being accidentally drunk as a teen to falling victim to paralytic fits a mere decade later and spraining my ankle on a night out. It's safe to say I've learned lessons of my own, and that's proba-bly why I stick to one staple in the present day – which, if you're new here, is red wine, specifically Merlot or Malbec if you're gifting. I suspect that almost everyone goes through seemingly endless teachings via varied spirits as a rite of passage. I mean, if you didn't almost die once at the hands of two bottles of rosé for a fiver, were you yet living? No, I'm not suggesting you actively damage your liver to prove my point, but the point here is that you're almost *supposed* to go through messy moments with alcohol to find out whether it's really for you or not. Again, please do not trial binge-drinking because I said to do so; I realise I'm a living breathing hypocrite and, much like the stunt warnings of *WWE*, I suggest you do not try this at home . . . unless supervised by a 'responsible' adult.

While drinking remains my second favourite activity – second only to curating playlists that no one really cares for – with it comes the ashamed aftermath and reaching for your phone to make sure it made it back safely with you in the Uber, and checking that you didn't leave your keys in the door . . . again.

Turning twenty-one is a huge milestone for young people, despite nothing really changing for Britons residing in the UK. We put such emphasis on this change in age and desperately want the celebrations surrounding the special date to be perfect. An old biddy by nineteen, I never expected my twenty-first to be a rager, as with my previous birthdays; my only wish was that I looked like a peng ting and had a good, cocktail-infused night's sleep. However, my friends were determined to create whole events surrounding their birthdays, and I greatly enjoyed them. I have an uncontrollable need to please people, sometimes at my own peril, and the same can be said of my attitude towards friends' birthdays. Desperate to make them view themselves as the main character for the day, month, YEAR, I feel it my duty to remind them that they were ejected from their father's scrotum in order to have whole months dedicated to the celebration of their birth.

I am the annoying friend whose sole purpose it is to remind you that you're the baddest bitch in the room. So, when a friend showed up with three people for her twenty-first birthday, originally expected to be a party of fifteen, I knew what I had to do. It was my turn to make sure my girl felt appreciated, loved and, most of all, absolutely obliterated by the end of it all. Although little of the confidence I encompassed in my early twenties lives with me today, a recently twenty-one-year-old me was more than charming enough to make sure we could make the best of a bad situation and collect as many free drinks (with no strings) as possible. Flirting my way into handsome men's conversations, I somehow managed to garner the interest of the club owner, who was more than happy to serve us for free for the entire night – which of course spelled trouble.

In likely my favourite drunken tale of my early twenties, despite us having an incredible night (remembered only via the few flash-backs we can piece together) the pair of us woke up in our respective homes each missing the items you're supposed to pat yourself down for when you enter the house. While I had somehow gotten home and managed to get back into my house, I had lost both sets of keys – for my family home and my university flat in Leicester – as well as a single shoe and various other items. My friend on the other hand had found my missing pointed ASOS pump, but had lost her phone, likely during her attempts to save my shoe falling out of the cab door. Hungover and slung over the toilet bowl the following morning, knowing the sacrifices it took to make that night a success, I questioned my choices from the night before. Soon enough, my phone flashed with messages from men I'd forgotten I'd even met.

Hey! Remember me from last night? read one. *Yo, Lauren . . . u good?* read another. These were the consequences of my overfamiliarity with bottle-serviced tables and the bar staff, and I hadn't the heart to block. Instead, I played the waiting game, hoping that my literal feeling-like-death causing my total silence and a lack of WhatsApp display picture updates would be enough to deter the interested parties looking to collect the debts of their bar services from the previous evening.

Counting the bruises I'd acquired the following day – likely from navigating my way out the club – I'm reminded that alcohol-related injuries are a staple of my nights out. Waking up to bruises of unknown origin and wondering why your face aches when you rinse off the dried drool stains, while chapped lips are also part and parcel of drinking beyond your means. Owner of one too many drunk injuries to count, I can admit that I should have been wheeled home from most events in a stretcher. Running and falling was my forte, as for some reason – and much like the current TikTok trend of testing one's endurance in heeled footwear – I thought it looked cute? Grazing my knee, spraining an ankle and getting a black eye at the hands of a heavy-duty door are just some of the effects of my nights out, making for hilarious stories some ten years down the road. Indulging in the stupidity known simply as 'enjoying oneself', we unlocked the sweet spot of not giving a fuck and using our durable young skin as a crash-test dummy.

Sitting in the driver's seat and speeding head first into a number of choices we'd come to later regret, the drunk version of us is powerful in its decision to try the inebriated version of Red Bulls flying with caffeinated wings. The lapses in judgement are due to alcohol's effect on the functioning of our prefrontal cortex, disrupting the decision-making process so we're free to act as stupid as we like with no immediate consequences.

DRINKING 'N' DATING

As you can imagine, dating is quite a difficult plight because I'm often the butt of jokes about being under the influence, which is fine. Men look at my drinking habits as Aiden did with Carrie's smoking habit – disgusting and something to be eradicated. Though Carrie's smoking habit *was* pretty gross, it was her habit to have. Aiden, who I've since realised wasn't wholly a Prince Charming, declared that he couldn't date a smoker, which is totally fair. But it's my understanding that smoking isn't a habit you can just 'give up' – you know, because of the whole nicotine thing. To give you a brief overview of the plotline that made me wary of tall, attractive men: Carrie declares that she will give up smoking (eventually) and instead focus her attention on the handsome six-foot man, which would be just as stupid in reality as it was in *Sex and the City*. Spoiler alert – the relationship doesn't last.

One of my best friends refuses to drink, and actively stopped the day I met her. Ironically, I was completely shitfaced. Till this day, she'll order a steaming pot of tea while the rest of us drink whole bottles of wine and gluttonously down overpriced cocktails. Having gone through her own life lessons, she came to the realisation that perhaps alcohol and drinking, for no reason whatsoever, just weren't for her. I commend her decision, and though I routinely rock up to her home with a solo bottle of red, she never passes judgement. She understands that my decision to drink doesn't mean that she has to, and vice versa. Some of the men I encounter, on the other hand, use every opportunity to police my habits. My non-judgemental demeanour means that I'm unfazed when dating avid potheads, but I am quite harshly critiqued if I exasperatingly scream 'Ugh, I need a drink!' to a new mate.

Over the past few years, I've been approached by a number of men who are against my drinking habits and rather vocal about it, as though me getting blackout drunk is an everyday occurrence. I mean, come on – moderation, lads! Blackout drunk is reserved for the weekend, at bottomless brunch, followed by afters at the closest 2-4-1 bar. Today, I can immediately tell when a prospective partner isn't for me. That man is usually disguised as my type on paper, but exposes himself by way of patronising 'I bet you're out drinking' text messages every so often.

I suspect the few men brazen enough to tell me that I drink 'too much' are unable to grasp the concept of drinking *casually*. I'm sure they likely envisage me smashing wine glasses on the floor and screaming 'ANOTHER!' like Thor; however, I find absolutely no fun in not being able to map my surroundings, or feeling dizzy and sick in the same breath – which should be a comfort to whomever I end up with in 2053.

Exercising control and knowing exactly when to hit pause – and yes, that's often when I feel like I'm floating while sat or laid completely still – I imagine they fail to understand my rather tame relationship with booze, and instead, choose to judge it as a result. The point being, I know exactly what my limit is, and though it's a struggle for many to grasp, I actually enjoy drinking – not to get absolutely obliterated, but just to sip and release prominent sighs of relief every so often.

For me, the overall concept of dating is rough. You're required to keep pressing the restart button on conversations about your child-hood, favourite films of all time and hobbies, which can often feel like rebooting Sims 4 without having pressed Save Game before shutting down the last time. Discovering a new person's habits and interests can be trying, as you don't yet know what you can and can't say in their presence – and the topic of alcohol is usually a sensitive one to take on. Especially for those of us who've made it a whole personality trait by accident. It's difficult for me not to express my love of wine because, even if I don't say it verbally, it's stated via the tattoos etched on my body – particularly the glass of red wine tattooed on my ribcage.

While many of my anecdotes are prefaced with the amount of booze my friends and I ingested on nights out, not everyone is privy to seeing the funny side of these stories. Instead, leaving room for awkward silence when the mention of my friends throwing up on public transport crops up and immediately letting me know that I cannot show them how I repurpose empty wine bottles as quaint home décor, I find dating quite hard in general. However, now that I'm older and a frequent wine drinker, I find it even more diffi-cult for some reason. Tales of falling over or being unable to locate my wallet the morning after read more as irresponsible than as the kinda-sorta adult who just likes to have a good time that I portray myself to be. Which means explaining the hilarious story behind my expensive new wallet becomes a bland tale of just needing an upgrade on my old one. But more than that, if I'm uncomfortable talking about something I enjoy without judgement, I feel as though I cannot fully be myself, and therein lies one of my difficulties.

Admittedly, I'm most comfortable in settings that involve a glass of something, as I find it easier to skip out of dates early when abiding by the rule of one drink maximum. This means I can use the excuse of only coming out for one drink to exit stage left in a hurry, should I detect no vibe at all. An action that has served me well on some truly terrible dates. Unlike disastrous dates experienced over dinner, where you find inappropriate images on their phone before the food has even arrived and must sit in awkward silence until such time when you can request to-go boxes and leave. Yes, this has happened to me.

Let's face it, the jungle – as it's referred to by those of us still experiencing the lions, tigers and bears on offer – is terrifying, and entering it without my suit of armour of a one drink maximum leaves me feeling even more vulnerable than I did when first agreeing to the date. Without bar dates I fear I'd be required to endure stale conversation topics during the dreaded talking stage without an exit plan in place, and I'm far too ill-equipped for that battle as it is.

THE DOS . . . AND THE DON'TS

Here's your entry exam for Drinking 101:

- DON'T mix wine and Hennessy, especially on an empty stomach – you WILL vomit and pass out in someone else's treehouse.

- DON'T go date drinking with someone who's driving. You will end up as the only person truly pissed, and you will do regrettable things that need not be written about.
- DON'T drink around people you dislike. You'll likely end up confronting them and well . . . yeah, just don't do it.
- DO eat before you go out, or you may risk projectile-vomiting in your friend's lap while on a packed Piccadilly line train.
- DON'T pair a boob tube with a bracelet that catches on everything for your birthday, when everyone will be paying for your drinks. The result is accidentally revealing your tits more times than you can count and traumatising your family members.
- DON'T drink so much that you need to pee, argue with the staff at McDonald's and then piss on the doorstep in protest when they don't let you inside to use the loo.
- DON'T get trashed on cheap wine. I don't remember why exactly, but the scars on my knees and under my eye say that you just shouldn't.
- DON'T attempt to show your 'party trick' to new audiences unless practised for your friends beforehand. If not, your pole-dancing routine may result in an embarrassing near-kick to a stranger's face.
- DO make sure you can handle your liquor enough that you don't pass out in someone else's bathroom.
- DO make sure there's a bathroom nearby the following morning if you've been on a raging bender.

The Writer on Modern Love

Chapter 3: The Writer On Modern Love

I couldn't help but wonder, was my love life panning out exactly like all the TV characters I swore blind I'd never become?

They say your first and sometimes the most important relationship with a man is the one forged with your father or father figure. Setting the precedent for how you interact in romantic relationships down the line, if those are with men, this first interaction affects whether you think all men are trash and capable of truly heinous things or whether you're a hopeless romantic and the Charlotte York of your friend group.

When I was a kid, my dad made me watch an episode of *The X-Files* that scarred me for life. While I was always his go-to for horror and thrillers, this one episode completely shaped how I slept at night going forward, as I would spend the rest of my days with the covers over my head to avoid alien life forms probing the back of my neck. I came to realise that a lot of my idiosyncrasies were developed in my formative years, many of which I carried with me through to adulthood and almost all of which were because of my father. To this day I still face a near-panic when I'm given thin sheets as they won't protect me against potential UFOs. Despite it not being a 'childhood trauma', it's worth noting that my father's efforts to include me in his love of the Syfy channel shows did little but make me all the more fearful of nonsensical paranormal happenings – and, in turn, in my future relationships with men.

As I've gotten older, I see more and more clearly the ways in which the odd relationship I have with my father may have affected the way I view men in general. While I may have been lucky enough to have a biological father present, his physical presence didn't necessarily 'give what it needed to give' and I was starving for some semblance of affection from that father figure. This missing daddy-daughter dynamic meant that I feared relying on men and trusting men as a whole, and this affected my future relationships, if we're being honest. It was only later that I learned what it meant to be reliant on a father figure, as I forged a new dynamic with my stepfather.

I'm sure someone will tell me it's typical of my star sign or whatever, but given that words of affirmation are my primary love language, harsh words have a tendency to stick to me in the worst of ways. Even when said in a humorous manner, I can't help but replay the words that left me feeling terrible about myself. And, of course, many of those came from my father. He made comments about my experimental (admittedly terrible) hairstyles and my choices in expressive clothing, which were influenced by my changing musical preferences. In writing this, I have just recalled the time where I was told to wear a vest underneath a long-length crop top, in an effort to suppress my bad bitch from the get-go.

Today, he often tells me that I'm beautiful when I update my display picture on WhatsApp, but I always go back to that one time when he called me ugly. Well, the one time he did it to my face in his home. Even though it was said in a 'joking' manner, I wanted to rid myself of my skin because I knew I was – and even with a layer of sarcasm in his voice, those words were not baseless facts.

Frequently experiencing flashbacks of some of the worst moments in my life thus far, all his subsequent compliments have felt like lies as a result. Sure, it was said as a joke of sorts, but at my lowest I always relay to myself the three words that reduced me to tears at a mere sixteen years old. Understanding that our daddy-daughter dynamic was a somewhat sarcastic one and lacking the words of affirmation I so desired, I began to view our relationship as perhaps him just not wanting *me* as a daughter. I longed to be adored in the same way he seemed to adore my cousins with longer hair and smaller noses.

Never truly feeling like a pretty young woman, I began hating myself and hating what stared back at me in the mirror from quite early on. These insecurities, which grew with me and followed my every thought, led to an influx of fleeting romantic relationships that I used purely for the bouts of instant gratification I craved from a father-figure. Following this instance (one I hadn't realised affected me as harshly as it did), my self-worth crumbled at the mere thought of anyone rating my appearance. I knew I wasn't particularly pretty at sixteen years of age, but to hear it from a parent, who is supposed to lie to you to tell you that you are anyway, shook my belief system to the core. Adopting the social distancing techniques I use to separate myself from my emotions, this played a massive role in the way I *un*wrote myself from my dad's life. Though I'm sure it was meant playfully and said in jest, the words '*you* are ugly' left me cold and wanting to run back to my mother's home a mere twenty-minute train ride away. His comment was unprovoked and I had always had an inkling that he felt this way, I just never expected to hear it. In all fairness, I considered myself to be ugly. The transitional years from ten to seventeen were rough, to say the least.

Not feeling peng enough for the boys my age was one thing. I was used to being part of a culture that favoured women of a certain look, not having the loose curls desired by boys in my age group. But this was a step too far for my lacking self-worth. Sometimes

I look at other girls and envy their relationships with men who've told them from the jump that they're perfect. Instead, my 'hero' was the first man to make me *really* question my appearance, and likely in the worst of ways.

It's contributed heavily to the way I believe men perceive me, and in general I think that the male gaze is a detriment to women's self-esteem. I've read a lot about the male gaze and how its perception warps how we feel about ourselves or view ourselves. While I'm sure most men believe we spend hours in salons shedding hair and applying extensions simply for their praise, these are acts carried out to improve the relationships we have with ourselves. Enjoying our reflections that much more post-glow-up, we're able to distance ourselves from feeling low. Growing up, many of my hair changes were likely made so that my father would notice me and adore me the same way I felt he did my other family members, but his commentary only made me feel worse and I soon stopped chasing that feeling, turning my head instead to boys my age and new heights in ruining my self-esteem. What a joy to be an ugly teen, eh?

Today, despite developing my mindset on this a little – and unlearning the feeling of 'ugliness' via my favourite TV shows, and navigating what it meant to glow up – I'm very aware of how these small factors growing up have massively contributed to the ways in which I view myself and my romantic relationships. My self-proclaimed daddy issues, although slight to many, have felt like a massive meteor in my world as I have been unable to accept compliments from a variety of people I believed to be lying. These minute factors from my childhood each contributed to how I treat my friends and other people around me now, as well as how kindly or harshly I treat myself.

This group of 'unconscious associations' known as the father complex have negatively impacted the way I approach men, as my first-ever association was the destructive dynamic formed with my father. It wasn't until my stepdad entered my life when I was twelve that I started to understand what it meant to trust and rely on a father figure, for which I'm eternally grateful.

Raising me up and reassuring me when I was at my lowest, by way of trips to the local Caribbean takeaway and in-depth discussions about my teen problems, my stepdad taught me there was another spectrum of men who didn't seem so terrible, and this later opened my eyes to the upside of romantic relationships. His congratulatory comments on major achievements and my being able to lean on him for advice relieved many of the tensions that had built up from having a dad who wouldn't just lie to me in order to raise me up. Even being patted on the head and told 'you're alright' – this affectionate act was enough to help me navigate a new father-daughter dynamic.

ROMANCE REALITIES VS. ROMANCE NOVELS

When I think about real, romantic love, I'm often slapped by the realisation that I don't really want it. Not really. I feel similarly to Drake on his track 'Connect', because for me the idea of a romantic partnership is always far more exciting that the actuality.

The idea of having someone is great, but the reality takes me back to being in Year 6 and my first middle-school relationship. I'll never forget the day; it's one that is permanently in my memory bank. The boy I'd been crushing on all year *finally* asked for my hand in playground marriage, via my best friend. Well, 'marriage' is a little strong, I was 'middle-school asked' to be someone's girlfriend and, of course, gushingly said 'YES' via a torn-off piece of paper. Only it was the *idea* of him that excited me. The reality was a growing realisation that men (boys) absolutely terrified me. I greatly remember spending the entire first day of our prepubescent relationship avoiding him, once I'd garnered the title of girlfriend. Looking back, I'm not entirely certain what it was that I was afraid of, I just knew that belonging to someone at that time was bizarre AF and even uttering a word to him meant that we were a thing, a notion I was unequipped to handle. I mean, WTF do you even do with a boyfriend? Especially at that age. Was he expecting to kiss at some point? Would we have to hold hands in the playground? Could I still secretly have a crush on the next victim, who I'd soon grow an inability to speak to once I became *his* GF? Even in my junior years, cynicism was rife in me and my anxieties clearly took centre stage.

I mean, how could I *belong* to someone? No longer would they refer to me as Lauren – I would henceforth be known as girlfriend of [insert name of my first 'boyfriend', whose identity I'll protect because he absolutely still follows me on social media]. For some reason, whenever I freak out about a relationship – any relationship – in the present day, I think back to that encounter with my very first he-who-should-not-be-named. As you can probably tell, I asked another friend to delete the relationship and tell my middle-school bae that it was over by 3 p.m. that very same day. My shortest-ever try at a relationship, and some might say the toughest – largely because it was my first. I thought of all the novels I'd read where they spoke of the spark of the first kiss, and I'd binge-watched episodes of *Bad Girls* and *Footballers' Wives* long after my bedtime, so I knew what a kiss was, I just wasn't particularly sure I wanted one just yet. Much less that I was ready.

My middle-school years were somewhat of a nightmare highlight reel, detailing 'what not to do' when it came to boys, and I only strayed further and further from actually getting a boyfriend going forward. Actions like asking whether or not someone was still into me fifty times a day, or writing long SMS paragraphs about how perfect we were together when clearly we were not, most likely did not help my cause.

Perhaps this was sort of my first try at self-sabotage. Like sure, why not choose the guy who has a giant crush on your mate and ask him out when you know he's about to ask her out? Self-sabotage 101, folks. I should have done something that made sense, but the false sense of security I found in heartbreak was my comfort zone – and I liked it there. As long as I was down in the dumps about an unrequited love, I could focus on my oddly specific poetry, obscene wall art, and the collages in the front of my schoolbooks that my teachers would often raise an eyebrow at.

Professing my love was carried out via poetry and various posters on my wall. Detailed rewrites of existing love songs with my crush's name instead of the word 'boy'. My crushes knew not the extent of my obsession. The soundtrack to my life at that time, Rihanna's 'There's a Thug in My Life', was rewritten several times to express my love for a certain adolescent. Changing the title lyric to 'there's a boy in my class', I embarrassed myself through song, and this private obsession would be just one of a plethora of awkward crush moments to come. At least this one was carried out in private and only heard by my mother when she dropped off the laundry at the foot of my bed.

My teen years were . . . um, tough, to say the least. The moment I heard that someone might have a crush on me, I'd ignore them until they inevitably got over said crush and I'd be utterly heartbroken after the fact. Then I'd settle into comfortable friendships and run scared if the topic of 'like-liking' me came up again. Always running away and afraid, I avoided nice guys like the plague and clung only to men who'd text me once a day to say *cum c me* but had very little interest in anything more than attempting to finger me in public spaces.

Though you're supposed to move on from this section of life, I fear that I'm stuck in a time warp whereby *I'm* now the guy texting once a day for just enough attention to tide me over. My adulthood dating experiences mirror my childhood crushes, so much so that

I find myself wondering what twelve-year-old Lauren might do in many of these instances.

Watching – or rather binge-watching – *Jane the Virgin*, I learned a few things, namely that I'm still grossed out by displays of affection when I'm not in 'like', and also that perhaps it's just a gene I'm missing? I mean, people often fall head over heels when potential suitors make grand gestures and clear their schedules for them, but for some reason those gestures simply put me on edge. When hearing about my friends being surprised by their husbands and boyfriends, I often look at those surprises as though they're an inconvenience. And here's where my love language struggles. Unable to let anyone in for more than a quick beer and a lipsing session, I see other halves as something of an accessory and not a need.

Cold-calling my Year 5 crush Daniel and experiencing that first brutal middle-school heartbreak was likely a cause of this fear of truly committing to anything that might make it past the three-month mark, and perhaps Daniel and his rejection are the real root of my commitment issues. Always taken back to the stark silence followed by the 'no thank you' response I was given, and how my nights were followed by Tynisha Keli's iconic 'I Wish You Loved Me' after that moment.

NEVER BEEN KIS— OH WAIT . . .

At fourteen years old I had about as much experience with boys as you might imagine a fourteen-year-old would have – none. In the early stages of my teenage years, when I was still navigating how to conceal my missing boob beneath my school jumper, my limited experience with boys only came to me courtesy of the TV shows I likely shouldn't have been watching.

In Year 9, and drowning in my Year 11-sized blazer, Adam told me he liked me. Like, to my face. As with my current encounters with men, I immediately questioned his comment with: 'You sure?' To which he nodded in confirmation. I would soon lose all sense, as the excitement of having a boy I kinda liked like me back was too much to bear. I was utterly obsessed with my teenage crush and long-time friend, who soon became the only thing I could focus on during school hours. Despite our rocky start, I couldn't understand or believe that this boy who spent his evenings calling and texting me to talk about pretty much nothing could actually like (*like*) me. Adam was everything a teenage girl could want.

This was brand-new territory, and the mere idea of a potential boyfriend excited me no end, despite my fear of actually having a boyfriend. That Friday afternoon, the forty-minute journey home from school no longer felt long, as I spent the entirety of the journey listening to Fantasia's 'When I See U' on repeat and imagining what our wedding might look like in the year 2009.

For a teen, he was gorgeous. There was just something about him, and everyone saw it. In my pubescent haze, his thick brown hair was all I could visualise while being taught mathematical equations I would never use in the real world. After all our MSN catchups, routine text debates and sporadic phone calls, he finally asked me out on a date. I say 'finally', but it would be my first-ever date and, of course, I had no idea what a date even entailed.

Much like the teen version of Channel 4's *First Dates*, it was every bit as awkward as one might imagine. Despite talking every day and being the best of friends before the fact, this first date felt like my first time talking to a human ever, and it was certainly my first in a 'romantic' setting.

Vue Cinema, Harrow, sometime in 2006 . . . I think Adam and I bought our first-date tickets to see DreamWorks' *Flushed Away*. When we sat down under the luminous, flickering cinema lights, he looked even cuter than usual and my crush intensified to full-blown like-*like*. He put his hand on my knee and stroked it with his thumb, presumably to provide comfort, but instead it only filled me with more fear about this actual romantic encounter. The film had yet to start when he leaned in and told me how pretty I looked (*LIAR!!!!!!*) and my nerves reached 99.8 per cent. I knew what was coming, despite my lack of knowledge in a dating capacity, because I knew from rewatching *10 Things I Hate About You* a million times over that a boy leaning in meant he was about to kiss you, but I was far from ready for this moment. It only took three more lean-in compliments before he gently grabbed my neck and planted one on me. My very first kiss. Unsure of whether or not I was doing it correctly, I remember just . . . *being* there, suspended in an awkward pouty stance, reminiscent of the awkwardness displayed in *The Inbetweeners*. Then the first kiss – or peck, rather – soon came to a close, and as our movie began, I could think of nothing else. This was enthralling (and just like a drug in liquid form I now indulge in), and I knew I was about to become horrendously obsessed.

Kisses two, three and four soon followed, but with tongue – and when I think back, I laugh. As it was of course my first kissing experience, I relied heavily on my crush to demonstrate what the fuck to do. Looking back, he was equally as clueless, as we just sort of . . . rubbed tongues? I dunno, it was weird. Soon enough, I was so enamoured with this individual that I could do nothing but obsess. In a parallel universe where I was Carrie Bradshaw and Adam was Big, I couldn't stop myself from gushing about his overall being to anyone willing to listen. But it was within this relationship that I learned boundaries, and where to draw the line on being Big-obsessed.

It only took about two months for the entire thing, and my entire world, to crumble. Soon enough, I'd fall victim to the ghosting saga we've all been privy to today, and would find out via Myspace that not only were we over, but he had also moved on. Fun for teen-me. This thrilling first teen love was so intense it dominated my metaphorical newsfeed for months. Well, it would have if we'd had live newsfeeds at the time. The rather public breakup left me scarred, and my entry-level exam in ghosting would set the tone for my love life to come.

HASHTAG JUST PLAYING THE GAME . . .

Let us circle back to the good years, and logging on to MSN in the hopes that your crush would be impatiently waiting online for your name to appear in the bottom-right corner of their screen. If they weren't online when you finally managed to log in using your dial-up internet connection, you'd hide offline for a little while longer, wait for *their* name to pop up and then make your grand entrance 2–3 minutes later, perhaps with a cute new mirror selfie or a flood of emoticons in your incredibly well-thought-out screen name. It was all part of the game – the chase, if you will – and this was just the start of our game-playing, though we may not have known it. We were inadvertently teaching ourselves how to play hard to get. I often question why, because at that time we were likely hard to want, and while we probably thought we were slick as fuck, our basic flirtation techniques consisted of colourful 'LOL' gifs in place of certain words, and changing our display picture every few minutes to show we were attractive at a number of different angles. Hey, everyone had to start somewhere.

Entering the dating pool at age 13/14, or rather the 'I like you, why don't you like me back' pool, was scary as fuck. Everyone had their own theory as to why the person whose name covered their schoolbooks wouldn't respond to their very obvious efforts in wooing. In fact, schoolgirl talks frequently consisted of commentary along the lines of 'Don't reply straight away – make him want you'. We teens were surely deluded, and the reason is probably the forbidden shows we binge-watched late at night, without any real understanding of their context. Hello *Footballers' Wives*. Not only that, but these teachings of how to lure the love of your life were in every sodding teen TV show and every after-school special. So why wouldn't we take those lessons into real life with us?

Did they work? No. But was that a lesson in itself? Hell, yes.

Soon enough, waiting for the love of your life to message you first on MSN transitioned into a newer and flashier way of pretending you weren't interested. No longer needing to screen your potential bae on MSN while waiting for the opportune moment to pounce into a flat-line conversation, you'd now progressed to not acknowledging their comment on the latest Myspace post but making sure to reply to everyone else's. Blatant and disrespectful, but it always sparked some sort of conversation – be it good, bad or just plain 'Wot, so u cnt reply to my comment nah?' But soon Myspace wasn't – for want of a better word – the 'space' for playing hard to get anymore. Now it was texting's turn to shine, leaving their message unread for several hours before sending the completely staged reply you'd tested with your bestie beforehand.[6]

As time passed, we all stopped texting and started on BBM messages, and purposefully leaving your crush's message unread but making sure to change your screen name a few thousand times in order to remind them that they were cute, yes, but you just weren't that into them . . . *yet.* Although you totally *were,* and it was killing you inside not to message the cutie in the Evisu bootcut jeans.

Later in life, and with technology moving forward, we moved from BBM screening – well, from BlackBerry phones in general – to

---

6   Side note: remember when you could mark your text messages as unread to make it look like you were more popular than you were?

screening WhatsApp messages. Oh yes. You know, before we knew what the blue ticks signified. Which brings us to today, using iMessage and purposely putting read receipts on to remind our prospective lovers that no one is really *that* important in the grand scheme of things, and yes, we've seen your message about not replying to your earlier message.

When you think about it, and I mean really think about it, modern love is a bit of a trip. I've been told a number of stories about my parents' love lives and the love lives of their parents, and I just think, *Fuck, shit is so different from today*. Sure, they were likely playing hard to get back then too, but when they got it, they were in it, even if that meant finding the love of their life when they were twenty years deep into a marriage with someone else (lol). Today, there are so many more pressures on us and a zillion more temptations. We're a far more exploratory generation, keen to test the waters in more ways than one, be it confronting our parents' toxic traits, quitting jobs after even the slightest bout of anxiety or trialling the intriguing porn videos we've seen online – whatever your vice. Being an adult and falling in love back in the day seems like it was miles simpler.

Now, I don't doubt that they had their own obstacles, but on the flip side, I also doubt very much that their relationship problems consisted of their beau double-tapping photos of attractive nude women on Instagram. Though I suspect that the olden-days version of this instance meant that partners may have found a nude magazine hidden underneath the bed and torn it to shreds in protest – you know, to remind their significant other that this is what would happen to their next £2.00 mag should they ever bring another into the household. Ballsy.

THE HOOD COMPLEX

My favourite part of teenhood is by far the 'government name' rhetoric. There was absolutely nothing more enthralling than dating a guy who detested people referring to him by his given name and instead only responded to his street alias. Take, for instance, someone who was far more comfortable being called 'Younga Stabz', despite never having held anything sharper than a butter knife. It was almost like dating a member of Anonymous.

What were his 'olders' like, and had they been part of a gang or were they, like Yung Skrilla, a fraud? Were you living if you hadn't been referred to as someone's 'bbz', all the while not knowing that his real name, his government name, was Darwin? Admittedly, I've had my fair share of redacted-government-name relationships, but I believe that to be just what life in the UK was about in the early 2000s. Being able to add 'WiiF3y Tiggz' to my MSN screen name meant that, despite not knowing, I really didn't care what his mother had named him at birth. For I could now create Photoshopped images where our photos overlapped one another, with graphic text and our names in unison. That was all that mattered now, not trivial conversations about his first name, surname and favourite colour. Something those dating in 2022 should take note of.

His little secret made the allure of having a boyfriend I couldn't bring home to my mother all the more fun. It also prompted me to again Rih-write the lyrics to Rihanna's 'There's a Thug in My Life' to better suit the situation.

Heavily been influenced by countless replays of hits on Channel U such as 'Gash by da Hour' and P2J Project's 'Hands in the Air', this was a time when everyone had a tag name for no real reason. They wore New Era caps cocked to the side and oversized T-shirts with whichever term was popular sprawled across in shiny lettering. With a grime track for quite literally everything, catchy songs perfectly accented enthralling summers spent at Hyde Park in large groups.

Starting out with small doses, our entry into social media (and its grossly misconducted, harsh grading systems) was via websites like Bebo. Ensuring that the world knew you were the creator of colourful profile skins, Bebo was our introduction to the pangs of social media. Through displayed details like 'other half', which was an option on the social media site at that time, we saw first-hand how selecting the wrong other half to link your profile to could be a detriment to your best friendships. If you were lucky enough to have a boyfriend aged fourteen, then you'd narrowly avoid all the drama surrounding selecting the wrong mate, as you could disclose that your hubby was your other half in MSN-style lettering saying ˉ"*º•.ˉ"*º• Wiifey Tiggz •º*"ˉ.•º*"ˉ next to his barely distinguishable profile picture. As you distributed 'luvs' and demanded you be sent one in return, your colourful profile was key to becoming popular online. But with only three 'luvs' to share between 120 friends each day, at least the madness was capped and it was vastly different to the scope of the scoring system of social media now.

Riddled with grammatical errors that would make me shudder now, our profiles were draped in falsified facts to make us appear more interesting online. We called ourselves names like *NW Pwiincess 2k7* and posted a number of weird, oversharing facts the internet needn't have known. We detailed our favourite tracks at the time in undetectable txt speech, and added a list of friends' names we 'luv'd', which usually included everyone you knew so as to avoid any tension from school friends and other peers. It was also not uncommon to decorate your friends' profiles with terribly drawn whiteboard art that would put your MS Paint attempts to shame, though I'm still not sure why this feature was ever a thing. Influenced by the favoured graffiti text that dominated the early 2000s, our homemade Bebo skins were cringy as fuck, and often along the lines of 'Bitch You Ain't God, So You Can't JUDGE ME'. How we've made it this far in the social media world without a fully fledged burnout is beyond me. We have digitally lived nine lives.

Categorising your Top 16 friends with cringe images designed specifically for this purpose, each had an arrow pointing at their profile declaring that they were 'peng-a-LENG' – like the 'I'm With Stupid' T-shirts couples purchase on holidays. Free to be as corny as we wished, we actually read the questionnaires our online friends posted detailing their crushes and their most intimate secrets. Long before LinkedIn, we'd declare how we knew someone via a tick box that, for some reason (Bebo???), questioned if we'd hooked up with or even knew them in real life. Which now, looking back, was slightly more intrusive than your rudimentary Instagram deep dive.

Learning to code via Tom's Myspace later, this slightly less intrusive site would still contribute to our feelings of inferiority online. Popular or not, we were subjected to ridicule if we selected the wrong few friends for our profile Top 8. Causing rifts and unmitigated controversies between real-life friends, the decision to place a celebrity in your profile was not one to be taken lightly. And I greatly remember having arguments over someone being moved from the first to the second row – I shit you not. Navigating the boundaries you could push online, it became all the more difficult to prioritise new friendships over old ones – and many felt as though they were left by the wayside due to their lack of skills in Myspace graphics.

The more you understood about coding, the better your chances of garnering new friend requests, as your skills in creating the most interesting profile to look at – through bold and italic texts superimposed on to selfies – would serve you well in gaining a larger audience. Among the common 'Showaman' tag, 'Oldaz' and 'Yungaz', it was your mission to be the coolest, most interesting profile to be friends with. Which meant taking selfies via small hand mirrors, just so you could include the back of the phone while attempting the perfect finger-to-chin shot.

FIRST LOVES ARE A BITCH, AREN'T THEY?

If there's one thing I wish I could do over, it would be to experience a first love again and relish that moment. This is mostly because I didn't actually realise I had fallen in love until it was over, and then I couldn't get over him.

We met for the first time in Barbados – my home, heritage and favourite country in the world. Like any fifteen-year-old, I was a miserable adolescent and my only interests included Ne-Yo's latest hit, boys and um . . . boys. So, naturally, John Doe 1 was among my failed conquests and right in my eyeline. Bored on my very first trip to Bim, he and I were both taken to the adult parties you were forced to attend because you weren't yet old enough to stay home alone. But John Doe 1's green eyes immediately caught my attention and I was left unable to speak, which was ironic for a kid who could never STFU. Poolside in my tortoiseshell H&M sunnies, swim shorts and tankini top, I avoided swimming so as to look cool – in the hopes that he would eventually come to me.

'John Doe 1, come and meet Lauren!' my stepdad shouted. John Doe 1 hopped out of the pool (he had been circling to catch glimpses of me) and flashed his perfect smile. New crush *activated*. The next few days we were pretty much forced to hang, but didn't get along at all. Reminiscent of our romantic relationship further down the line, we bickered and pissed one another off at every opportunity. But because of my love of misunderstood men, I longed for more and used the small pointless arguments about which song had more prominence in the UK chart as an excuse to keep us talking.

Whenever I recall my first-love story, knowing that I somehow fell in love at fifteen with a guy who showed little to no interest in me, I'm asked how the fuck I knew. I just did. I often chased the feeling of an unrequited crush (usually with celebrities), but this time it felt different.

Though we always crossed paths at family events going forward, something about our next encounter set a new tone for our budding romantic partnership. Three years later, at a wedding, I somehow grew the balls to ask the object of my three-year-long love outside for a 'quiet conversation', where I planted my lips on his. Eighteen now and sure of what I wanted, I wasn't going to allow petty heartbreaks from my earlier teen years to screw this up. From that first kiss came a million more, and soon we became inseparable. Lying to my mother about my whereabouts (sorry Mum!!!!) I'd sneak over to his home in North London just for a lipsing session and inappropriate, but relatively PG, cuddles. I was obsessed with him and he knew it, so I kept this love affair from everyone. He was my favourite and best-kept secret, and I spent every waking moment fantasising about our future together. The love story of the family friends who knew each other from fifteen years old. Until, of course, my Friday night sleepovers at Kizzle's became too much of a frequent occurrence, and the two-hour journey home made little sense as the friend's home I lied about staying at was a total of twenty minutes away.

Besotted and happy to admit to it, I did everything in my power to show John Doe 1 just how much I adored him, taking him to Arsenal football games and ordering takeaway from his favourite Chinese restaurant. However, the bickering of our formative teen years would be what rear-ended us at 18+. I was dirt-broke and my partner would consistently remind me of the fact, routinely making comments about how reliant I was on my parents and how I could only really get jobs that required short-term contracts – which, when looking back, were some of the happiest days of my life. A life free of unexpected bills, and a general disdain for adult responsibilities.

Being hard on myself, I began to refuse the help of my parents, making navigating my years at university and thereafter very difficult. Even refusing to have my driving lessons funded, I declared full independence at eighteen – and for what? For an insecure boy?! It was here that I realised that trying to 'make it on my own' at such a young age was to my detriment, and I now know that his attitude to me having help may have come from jealousy. But that was just one factor in what would eventually break us up – little by little the overall allure of the 'first love' began to fade, and I was utterly heartbroken before we eventually split.

Our love, once shiny and new, began to feel like a scratched CD that jumped on your favourite song. University meant that while we'd kinda-sorta decided to make things official, our already shaky bond would be tested by distance. I spent many of my last Friday evenings before uni holed up at his house. I could already tell that our relationship was going down the shitter, and I wanted to enjoy the last few moments before we flushed it away entirely. Promises of visits to my student quarters in Leicester soon turned into 'next weekend!' which soon turned into me travelling all the way back home just to see my beau. We bickered like the two kids who'd met on that trip to Barbados, and while the love was very much still present, so was a growing resentment. Sure, he called me his girlfriend in front of his best friend and drove me home to Leicester that one time, but these gestures felt empty and fruitless as we were both exhausted by each other.

I spent many of my nights in my first year of uni crying into rum-doused Häagen-Dazs ice cream and annoyingly texting him, *but are we okay?* before eventually calling it quits sometime before I went home for the summer. But this wouldn't last, as even with the hotties I flirted with on yet another family trip to Barbados, I couldn't rid myself of this first love. It was unshakeable, and I genuinely pondered if perhaps I might've had some sort of illness. Sick with love – how gross. I spent my nights crying over this mutual decision and used the post-breakup period to treat other boys as badly as I felt about losing my first love. Eventually, I caved, and on day four of the family vacay, I called to tell him I missed him and that Bim just wasn't the same without him. It was like nothing had changed. We agreed to meet after the trip and I was filled with glee at the thought of reconciling in my rather destructive relationship. We would be us again, and I couldn't care less about what my friends thought about our mismatched personalities or his inability to compliment me more than once a month. But I was basically dating my dad. The breakdown of this relationship broke me in more ways than one, because while I believed us to be back on track, he was holding in a secret that would blow my fairy tale to smithereens . . .

SOCIAL LOVE . . . ANXIETY?

I'll never understand why I allow social media to have such power over me, as my self-consciousness skyrockets when online. It's self-defeating and incredibly unhealthy, but I still subject myself to more of the same, even though I'm someone who crumbles at the sight of anything even remotely uncomfortable. I know, it makes very little sense.

The first time I ever deleted an Instagram account was the day John Doe 1's child was born. I remember it like it was yesterday. I liked the photo out of courtesy, commented my congratulations, and proceeded to delete the app so I could cry for several hours in my university flat. It still upsets me that I gave one photo so much power and found it impossible to scroll online without feeling inadequate. I felt worthless, and it was all the more pathetic because it was at the hands of someone else's good news. I soon realised that it wasn't enough just to delete the app from my phone; I decided to go back and really fucking take action. That night, I removed my account altogether and felt free(r). Though I still spent the evening in floods of tears, I felt significantly better about my situation. I mean, yeah, I was a pathetic sobbing mess, but at least I didn't have to see anything else to further that depressive mood. This process of deleting, deactivating and switching off from the online world soon became my living and wellness routine.

I think I created and deleted three Twitter accounts and two Instagram accounts before my friends intervened, sat me down and said that they'd refuse to follow me again should I create yet another profile. I listened, and after that, whenever I felt low, I'd either log out or simply deactivate for a while. Problem solved. It was definitely an unhealthy cycle, and unhelpful to the situation my brain constantly found itself in, but it was the only workaround I could drum up. I didn't want to be completely off the grid, but I wished to be off it enough that I didn't have to see things that bummed me out.

Just as quickly as the relationship with my first love began, it ended. I tried my best to get over (what I thought was) the love of my life having a child – and not with me – but I couldn't wrap my head around the concept of being someone's stepmum at nineteen. Still tied to getting blackout drunk by way of tequila shots, I struggled to fit a child into this routine on my mood board and so had to bow out. The tombstone had been carved, and we were no longer.

THE L-WORD = LOSS

Even though I've experienced losing people, there have been two prominent instances that affected me most in terms of grief: the losses of my grandmother and my best friend.

Despite experiencing my first real romantic heartbreak at nineteen, a bigger heartbreak was soon to follow. Yazzaman and I had known each other our entire lives, despite a troubled beginning. We were forced to be friends at age seven or eight, as her mother graciously took me in after school until my mother could pick me up. Our mothers were good friends by way of the school gate, so it only made sense that my school arch-enemy would become my after-school pal. Despite our playground rivalry, I enjoyed her company, though I didn't dare tell my peers for fear of a scolding for fraternising with the enemy. Further down the line we put aside our differences and I spent most days, nights, weeks at her house round the corner from my Harrovian flat. We were inseparable. She was the only person I could tell my secrets to; I spared few of the details and saw her as the much prettier version of myself. By age sixteen, we became friends out loud and just by association she elevated my social status from bullied weirdo to kinda cool, I guess?

Yazzaman was the reason I returned to school (somewhat) full-time in Year 11, post-bullying. She had the kind of confidence I could only dream of. Little by little, she restored some semblance of confidence in me, as she routinely reminded me of the power of positive affirmations: I had to think I was beautiful so that other people would think I was beautiful too. Our history of turbulence was completely erased and she became the only person I felt I could rely on – my real-life Girl Tech Password Journal. Our falling out is up there as one of the worst moments of my life because it happened mere weeks before my world collapsed around me.

At nineteen, I lost my best friend to a complicated illness. When I heard the news, I lost the ability to speak and my world turned completely black. Ever in one another's pockets, life without her felt like a punishment for putting myself first this one time after a rather pointless argument. *Why didn't I go round there and laugh it off like I usually did? What stopped me this time around?* Questions swirled in my brain as I tried to understand how being stubborn aided me in any way. I had just lost my best friend, and every day after the fact I was riddled with guilt for not having picked up the phone to make up, squash the beef and call her a dickhead because I missed her so much.

Since then, I've been almost overbearing in my friendships. Terrified of losing another staple in my life, my compulsive nature took centre stage and I prioritised those I adored most – even if it was to my detriment. At first, I believed a gratuitous love in my friendships to be completely normal, but after therapy, I understand how this might not be so.

To cut a long twenty sessions short, my then-therapist explained that my unhealthy attachment issues towards my friends were a direct result of losing a friend in that way. She informed me that, while my heart may have been in the right place, this unhealthy attachment style and attempting to gain control of uncontrollable situations meant I was adding to my anxieties – which consisted of a fear of the unknown and not being able to take control. Like many of my traumas, this is one that still affects me today, and while I've since found ways to deal with the grief of losing a friend prematurely, it has absolutely affected my view of relationships. Particularly romantic relationships, ironically.

Grief is one of those weird things that you feel unable to work through, despite everyone telling you that it takes time for the wounds to heal. I think that's just a lie to comfort those in distress, and it isn't very helpful. You can never really come to terms with loss; you just sort of learn to pocket it so that it doesn't consume you.

SWIPE RIGHT IF YOU FANCY

Much like the Barbies I had two of due to a messy divorce and my parents' lack of communication, my best friend Clare was like a shiny new toy. Mint condition, her fiery red hair lit up an otherwise dull and dreary office space. We met at my first postgraduate job and she immediately tickled my fancy, as she was the only other person at the office my age. Spending our lunch breaks devouring overpriced city lunches, we'd exchange phones and swipe right for the lols. What seemed like a desperate and dangerous game played over subpar Caesar salads had quite a high success rate, as many of the matches set me up for an excess of dates with a fair few London hotties. Still deadened by my first love, I used this period in my life to explore what I liked, didn't like, and what could be potential material for my writing.

I'm assuming that we've all acted like total assholes in a bid to mend a broken heart, and my early twenties were chock-full of meaningless interactions. Swiping through Tinder was my favourite pastime at twenty, and the reason was simple: because it meant finding someone hot, who also found you hot, and who could potentially fund your evening with a round (or six) of drinks. The perfect source of instant gratification, these pointless interactions were just the confidence boost needed after having my heart ripped out and tossed to the ground, and I became addicted to the feeling of being wanted. I broke down the awkwardness felt on many of these dates on my Blogspot, often divulging the nitty-gritty sexcapades on the rare occasion I sexperienced one. Headlining cringe blog posts with titles like 'Don't Shag the Help' and 'Help! I'm a Logophile', no details were left unsaid, making my dating life both interesting and a little awkward, as potential suitors begged me not to divulge the intimate details of our date once they found my online diary. At this time, while I was no closer to being in a committed relationship, my parents placed bets on how long each tryst would last, as I grew tired of every new guy I allowed to pick me up from my home address.

In my humble opinion, I was the most basic being and had no idea why I was getting any male attention at all. Still, I relished it, donning my Autumn/Winter Zara sale items and pretending to have some semblance of style. It had to have been the confidence in my Medusa-like gaze that lured them. Ensnaring them in my Venus flytrap, before turning them to stone with my newly adopted cold-heartedness, I loved the sense of control I had over these men my age (and often out of my league, at the time) who I demanded pick up me and my friends from random locations or guilted into ordering my favourite foods.

My obsession with facial hair saw me date a variation of the same man throughout my year of being twenty-one. Bearded hipsters were my prey of choice, and one particular conquest knew it. Let's call him Jake. Jake was a beautiful model whose DMs I boldly slid into. Similarly to Clare, his red hair caught my attention and I was ready to risk it all. Our first date went swimmingly. He met me at a pub near my workplace in Farringdon. One bevvy down the pub turned into five and we began planning our (very short) future and painting a vivid picture of the dates to come. This whirlwind love affair was likely the most exciting of that period in my life, because it went beyond just attraction and the ability to dissociate to a level of kinda-sorta like. Perhaps him being a 'we' guy was what swayed me, but I could do little but envision a future with this man – our careers mapped out and all. I should have known it wouldn't last, as any time I tend to visualise romantic partnerships beyond the haze of a first date, things always go tits up.

Jake and I hung out about twice a month, and the only reason I can recall this detail is because we always met either as I was about to get my period or while I was fully crossing the Red Sea. Mother Nature's cruel intentions to keep me away from Jake's nether regions, despite his advances, were probably a saving grace, as he later turned out to be a complete wanker. In a rather abrupt and volatile ending, Jake called one night to tear me a new one. In a time where Tumblr and Instagram were interchangeable, I'd made a grave error in judgement. I'd subscribed to a whole host of beard-specific accounts that posted pictures of hot bearded men from all walks of life, and I'd saved a photo of a man that made me utter the word 'oouuuffff' out loud. 'One like this pls', my Instagram caption read, and then I received a call and was told about myself from toe to toe. An otherwise quiet lad, my male Ariel had found his voice, and was using it to tell me that the hot unnamed man from Tumblr was in fact a close model friend of his. After a vigorous telling off, he asked if I had anything to say and I responded, 'I mean, he is hot, sorry!' I knew it was wrong, but by this point in our futile relationship I was bored stiff by his indecisiveness and this seemed like a get-out-of-jail-free card.

Somewhere in my blogging prime, this story was detailed in full, as I saw it as a step closer to becoming London's own Carrie Bradshaw, and now had one more failed situationship stamped on my dance card. Into the bin he went, along with the other men who had little impact on me and whose names escape me in the present day.

THE BREAKUP
THAT NEARLY BROKE ME

A modern fairy tale, John Doe 2 and I met at London Fashion Week as I dodged his camera shots much like Neo in *The Matrix*. Deathly afraid of the clarity of a Canon camera lens, I was there not only to review the designer shows but also to hold the bags of my counterparts while they had their ensembles papped by an onslaught of flashing cameras. I enjoyed this role; it helped me to feel safe and made for the perfect excuse when I was asked, 'Can I take a quick sna—?' Politely declining by raising one of three handbags and mouthing the word 'sorry', I felt a sense of comfort on the sidelines.

John Doe 2 was cute and very funny. I spent the remainder of the day bantering with him between shows and declining his advances . . . in trying to take my photograph. I saw nothing more than a budding friendship – but given that my previous relationships had developed from friendships, I probably should have seen it coming.

Soon enough, he and I became incredibly close. We'd spend our after-work evenings at Starbucks drowning ourselves in white hot chocolates and dishing on my dating life, my failed writing career, and all the jazzy work he'd been doing as a freelance whatever-he-was. He was my friend, and absolutely nothing could change that. Writing him into my life, as I did with many new friendships, I introduced him to everyone and no one could put their finger on why we weren't dating. But I had other plans – ones that included Friday nights sharing phones with my other friends and swiping right on unsuitable men. At twenty-one, taking dating as a joke and still plagued by the heartbreak of my last relationship, I had no desire for anything serious. But more than that, I didn't want to lose my best friend, and I absolutely would have, given the mind games I played with men. (Sincerely, if we dated when I was 19–22, I'm sorry. I've tried to recall the names of those of you who paid for the drinks of me and my pals, or who picked us up when we couldn't afford a cab home, but your names escape me. So, a universal 'soz', innit.)

So, on my end, there was nothing more than friendship. Despite him being handsome and hilarious, I had a mental block when trying to envision myself kissing him, though this was likely due to the idiot I was *actually* dating at the time.

On one of our many evenings spent frolicking around Shoreditch for overpriced drinks, he tried to kiss me and my body froze in the moment. He had broken the friendship barrier, and I had no idea how to work around this. *His lips are soft*, I thought to myself, *but this is weird and I'm going to fuck it up*. Quickly pushing him away before uttering the words 'dude, you ruined it', I ran to the Audi parked on the corner – occupied by one of the men I was dating at the time – which was my free lift home. Mysterious Mr. Audi hammered on about how much of a heartless prick I was on the forty-minute car ride, while I could do nothing but sit and take it or risk having to walk home from East to North West London. But I couldn't get my head around that first kiss. Then John Doe 2 texted: *SORRY! I've fucked it haven't I?*

He absolutely had. I replied that things were pretty weird now, as I couldn't do the whole friends-with-benefits but just-with-kissing thing. This wasn't a British teen movie, for Christ's sake. However, I later came to my senses, curious about whether or not it was the alcohol or had his lips really been *that* soft. So I called him over to hang in my front room with an Indian takeaway and the promise of whatever crappy show we were binging at the time. Within an hour I was keen to test the waters and face-planted on him. After a thirty-second kiss, I followed up with the fact that I'd just wanted to see what it felt like, for real. I wasn't lying, and I sort of envy myself at twenty-one because I haven't the balls to pull that stunt in the present day. The kiss was nice, but I wasn't quite ready to offer my ring finger and exchange vows so I carried on with my bullshit, ruining men's lives in lieu of therapy over John Doe 1.

To my knowledge, I've only been in love twice, and the first was probably what held me back the second time around. But that's silly, right, to blame someone who likely didn't realise just how much he'd affected my world, for my own mistakes in the future? I used to say that my first real heartbreak with John Doe 1 was the reason I was becoming a strong independent woman who didn't need no man, but the reality was that it had fucked me up so much that I was now void of any real emotion. I pushed away anyone who tried to love me because I imagined I'd end up the same weak-willed human I was at the close of that relationship. I also pushed friends too hard, and when they wronged me, I closed myself off completely. I treated men like props, because as long as they were at arm's length, things never had to be 'too' serious. It completely ruined my outlook on the world. In my view, not only were men trash, but the world and everyone in it too. Looking back, it wasn't the best way to handle situations, and likely led people to act in the same way I did to the people they chose to date after me. 'Oopsy Daisy' (no Chipmunk).

When I met my second love, John Doe 2, I didn't know what it was even though I'd been in love once before. Then it hit me like a ton of bricks, and I was so angry with myself for letting someone new love me, as I had foolishly convinced myself that my early twenties would be better used to work on and fix myself. I wasn't yet whole enough to allow someone real in. Somehow, even knowing the real me, he'd broken down my walls enough to get in and thaw my icy heart, and I felt fraudulent. I couldn't quite understand why, and so I pushed him away until I could push no longer. This feeling of not being ready is not one that's lost on me, as it's how I conduct many of my relationships.

Because of our year-long friendship foreplay, somehow I didn't realise how perfect the relationship was when we eventually started it. Sometime in March, he asked me to *officially* be his girlfriend, and I felt physically sick. Not because of him of course, but at the idea of being someone's girlfriend again. The concept had officially become dead to me, and I was more comfortable being the friend of someone I did everything with and also boned from time to time. That title-less period of time was my favourite, because it's the only time in my life I can recall being comfortable with the unknown.

He did relationship things like Valentine's Day, while I shuddered at the thought of actually celebrating. Perhaps similarly to the Grinch and his affliction around Christmas, it was just something I'd always cared very little for. Never really a big fan of red, the overkill displayed online on the 14th was something I wish I'd been diagnosed colour-blind for. Yet, wanting to please the man who did literally everything for me, I gave in a little and compromised for someone who loved a day I despised. I found new ways to keep us both happy and celebrate what I regarded as just another day in the month.

Growing up, Valentine's Day had never particularly affected me. As a pretty ugly kid, I humbly accepted my role as friend and messenger for each of the couples 'in luv'. I liked it there; it was a safe distance, and I could observe the couples who kissed in secret passageways so as to avoid being told to stop by the teachers.

It wasn't until Year 5, when a foreign exchange student told a friend to tell a friend to tell me that he liked me, that I saw *something* in a day designated for confessing your love for someone. Not much, but something. Though that's not to say I expected anything; having grown up plagued by daddy issues, I accepted from a very young age that men were prone to doing the bare minimum, even on days they were meant to shower you with love. This may also have been due to my early crushes unequivocally stating that they had no interest in me and never ever would.

My nonchalance about St Valentine only increased as I grew older. With a boyfriend on my arm but with almost no one knowing John Doe 2 existed, I still didn't see it fit to celebrate a day where love was the focal point. Despite all of this, I wanted to give my partner a morsel of the adoration he gave me, so I created the perfect workaround for V-Day for the two of us. Instead of celebrating our love for each other on the 14th, we'd celebrate on the 15th and declare it 'Anti-Valentine's Day' – music to my ex-emo heart. Despite its many similarities to Valentine's Day, this would be a day to be completely nonsensical, gifting novelty presents, playing drinking games and exchanging ridiculous cards. For me, this was perfect, because I was so anti about celebrating a day that made single people feel inferior – instead nothing was posted on social media, and we could just enjoy the idiotic yet thoughtful things we did for one another. Again, I'm well aware of the similarities to V-Day itself, but for me this was perfect as my major issue with the official day was that it was paraded about online and felt a little tacky.

OH SHIT, HE'S BACK-*BACK* AGAIN

Three and a half years, countless baecations and two volatile break-ups later, John Doe 2 and I were over. Similarly to the Carrie and Big saga, our relationship was so beyond done that it needed a new term to illustrate that fact. I'd always likened myself to Miranda Hobbes in *Sex and the City* – despite her being wildly successful and of course having striking red hair – and the reason was that we were both incapable of admitting when we were in love. Deadened inside by past relationships, we were one and the same. But making it in the end like her and Steve isn't always the outcome in reality, and it certainly wasn't for me.

What I've learned over time is that getting back with an ex is a lot like having your favourite contestant voted back on to a TV show after three weeks of absence. Sure, you're rooting for them or whatever, but you cannot confidently judge their whole performance as they haven't yet completed the toughest challenges and are basically picking up where they left off when they were eliminated. The same is true of relationships, because you missed out on many of the factors that shaped how you felt about them.

At first, the feeling of familiarity fills you with excitement and glee, because the person who once filled all your holes has returned to remind you that the feelings are reciprocated. But then dread enters the chat. You're immediately reminded of what happened and why you decided to part ways in the first place. (I'm certain there are hundreds of TikToks about this.) Likely because of past errors and/or the thought of all the new genitals they experienced while the two of you weren't together, something is always slightly askew . . . and you're both well aware of the fact. Despite onscreen depictions of reconciliations being cordial and seemingly easy to achieve, the reality is often anything but. I'm sure we all wish it looked about as hot as Brad and Jen's brief 'Hi Aniston, hi Pitt' encounter, however it's often less so.

Personally, I'm incapable of reconciling with exes, and I have tried and tested this twice over. Though I often feel like it's what I want, I'm immediately reminded of the overwhelming anxiety that plagued me while I was coming to the close of a partnership. Every time their interest dwindles even a little, I'm reminded that they binned me once and could decide they're through with me once again. Bored of rewatching their favourite series for the fourth time over, *Relationships* sponsored by Netflix presents them with a new and exciting show that pries them away at the fourth season and the episode about our reconciliation. (POV: I'm also the album they once had on repeat and had conveniently forgotten about, until I appeared on their Spotify shuffle at random.)

Unable to fully believe a man when he tells me that things are exactly as they are, I find more comfort in reminding myself that I was loved twice – and twice was enough. Perhaps you're only supposed to get one or two loves and that's it. Some learn this early on and hold on to their person tightly, while the rest of us squander the feeling out of fear and think to ourselves after our first loves, *Well, we had it once, so perhaps I can have it again.* Those of us who are the latter are opportunistic idiots.

We rewatch our favourite onscreen pairings rekindle their relationships, in awe of their perseverance, but the reality is more trying mercilessly to get over the thought of them having been with other people in your absence, and wondering about the new techniques they picked up during your absence. Loving in new and fandangled ways after getting back together, you're both well aware of the break and how it shaped the pair of you individually. Perhaps having developed a new sense of self-worth, you're never the same people when you get back together. And fictional romances are just that – fictional, and completely unlike my real-life love story.

110

Once John Doe 2 and I had officially ended our three-year-plus relationship, I didn't know what to do with myself. I felt quite literally like a part of me was missing. Amy's heartbreak documented via *Back to Black* felt not unlike my own. 'Tears Dry on Their Own' quickly became the soundtrack to my life, as what was once simply a playful melody I sang and danced to in my bedroom became lyrics I couldn't shake. Spending whole weeks in my friends' homes to avoid any *feeling*, my post-breakup therapy was avoidant *detachment*. And, I guess, actual therapy. Once again removing social media apps from my smartphone, and changing my username from *lawrenrae* to *imnotawriterrr* in a bid not to be found by him or his friends before doing so, I wanted to be perceived as little as possible.

Logging back in after six months or so, at first I tried my best to steer clear of *that* section of my Instagram account. I didn't bother to acknowledge it, because if I didn't look, it couldn't hurt me. Much like with the monsters I thought hid under the bed when I was a child, I convinced myself that not looking would allow the problem to die out. Old photos of us made me sick and routinely reminded me of the poor decisions I made at that time. So, the rule was: out of sight, out of mind. While our love affair was beautiful and apparently #goals, the aftermath was anything but. Because of our hypervisibility on the net, it was probably the hardest breakup to get over. I couldn't google my name without photos of us showing up as the top search, and was frequently asked 'Where's John Doe 2?' any time I dared to venture out alone.

With my anxiety at its peak, my social life pretty much crumbled as I struggled to enjoy a panic-attack-free night if I caught a glimpse of anyone that looked even slightly like *him*. Grabbing my life by the balls and finally taking action, I saw this as a call to get my shit together and actively get over the heartbreak. I began to put more effort into my appearance on the off-chance I might bump into him at the club, enquired about having braces fitted, and signed up for a gym membership on my mother's credit card.

Probably the most time I've ever spent in a gym, my mourning and my 'revenge body' goals kept me working out morning, noon and night, so I could feel the pain of anything but my heart aching. Setting my sights on abs, despite the improbability of anyone seeing them outside of beach bikini shots, soon enough I was confident enough in my own figure to push myself back into the dating sphere. Well, I attempted to. Because even after nine months of heartache, I cried at the first, second and third hurdles when a potential new mate awkwardly leaned in and tried to kiss me. But despite this, in putting the pieces of myself back together and thrusting my flat ass back into the world of dating, I gained a sense of self-confidence – the kind you read about in books. This new-found self-confidence saw me travel the world alone, accepting datecations from the men I crushed on and just generally not caring enough to place romantic partnerships at the centre of my life anymore. It took just a year before I felt like myself again and my *imnotawriterrr* alias became my full persona – after which this book was born.

Putting yourself first is important, as the romantic relationship you forge with yourself is the one that truly matters. This is because, despite our love of romantic partnerships, we are the only person we wake up to. You have to learn to appreciate the person standing before you when you wash your face in the mirror every morning before you can embark on new partnerships.

Word to Jaheim – because yes, it's important to put that woman before everyone else. And by 'that woman', he meant you, sis. Navigating singledom today, I understand that my feelings and self-worth matter more than proudly exclaiming I have a partner. Placing your needs before anyone else's might sound selfish, but it actually helps everyone in the long run as you're able to find your own self-worth before appeasing someone else's.

Challenging myself to read again as a means of post-breakup recovery, I picked up a book my mother gifted me when I was in a relationship, entitled *The 5 Love Languages: The Secret to Love That Lasts* by Gary Chapman. No longer feeling uneasy at the idea of eventually ending up with someone, I opened it up and learned many (many) things about myself and how I love. Or rather, how I would love again in the future. I immediately grabbed a pen, and little by little I began to forgive. Forgive myself for my errors, forgive someone I'd loved for his, and forgive those I had even a slight interaction with over the years who'd wronged me. I often forget the healing power of words, despite words being my coping mechanism for most things, but I stayed up that night until 5 a.m., reading, writing and understanding.

My new knowledge would serve as an SATs test for future relationships, and help me navigate the similarities and differences between my partner and me. Enabling me to relearn how to love and what it means to be open enough to love, this book acted as my guide for what to do going forward. Identifying not only my own primary love language but also the potential love language of my next partner, the book opened my very closed-to-love mind and helped me to understand where I may have gone wrong in previous encounters.

In short, Chapman details that there are five primary love languages, and there's a test that indicates which best applies to you. The five languages are: words of affirmation, where I heavily reside; quality time; physical touch; acts of service; and receiving gifts. Before taking the test, I had always assumed that my only language would be acts of service, however my being starved of words of affirmation confirmed where I might have gone wrong in dating men who could not eke out a simple compliment. Understanding that these love languages affect many aspects of life – and not just romantic partnerships – I began to better understand why I had always been so hurt by the comments of others, and why those ill comments lingered in my mind for so long after the fact. This helped me to better understand not only how things affected me, but also the way I approached other people. I thought about how often I complimented my peers and even strangers, and my primary love language of words of affirmation made all the more sense because it gave me a reason as to why I was so complimentary of people: it was something I craved in return.

This concept is not unlike getting back into the dating game after a truly catastrophic run of relationships. Getting back on the horse, so to speak, is a difficult thing to come to terms with. Tattooed with battle scars from previous interactions, you have to learn how to take life lessons forward, and in a slightly different way than you do with your fears. Trying not to paint new partners with the brush of the old ones is the trick, and often something I myself struggle with. Using life lessons as a guide to what not to do while exploring new interactions can help you find a balance between being street smart and being vulnerable enough to open up and try new things. Plagued by many of the interactions of my past, and more often than not having experienced the same situation multiple times over, this is one I'm still adjusting to as I subject myself to new people in the dating pool.

FRIENDSHIPS ARE LIKE LONG-TERM RELATIONSHIPS

To paraphrase Gretchen Wiener from my favourite teen flick, friendships are just as cute as relationships, people totally like friendships just as much as they like relationships, and when did it become okay for one type of relationship to become the boss of all relationships? WE SHOULD TOTALLY JUST HAVE BOTH!

Learning the intricacies of adult friendships is no easy feat. Though many of us believed the friendships we made at twelve would carry through to our thirties and beyond, we couldn't have been more wrong. Whether it was losing friends to new partners, idiocy, babies or marriage, none of us were fully equipped to handle the trials and tribulations that came with growing up and needing to distance ourselves from people we never believed we'd stray too far from.

We talk about them often – friendship breakups, that is – and while they can feel every bit as awful as the end of romantic relationships, we don't necessarily examine the scars we're left with post-breakup. Waking up sans friend, the post-breakup haze following a friendship fallout is a pain like no other. Unlike romantic entanglements, there's something almost eerie about no longer having the person you spend all your time with there anymore. I've experienced friendship breakdowns, and many were my own doing. There's a learning curve in how to process who is for you and who may have never been, and I understand that there's a lesson behind every person placed in your life. Except, perhaps, short-term situationships, which I sometimes believe should be abolished.

TV shows like *Friends*, *Sex and the City* and *Girlfriends* were key in portraying adult friendships as effortless and not needing too much work. While there is some truth to these depictions, given that we're all busy with something – such as children or drowning in a deep depression – certain aspects of our friendships still need to be tended to.

Having spent an inordinate amount of time researching how to maintain adult friendships, I don't think there's a secret formula. Perhaps it's like my good friend Sharkanna says: some people just aren't supposed to be in your life for an extended period of time.

Overstaying your welcome in a friendship is much like the morning after the night of a raging bender with a one-night stand, and perhaps there is a time limit placed on particular friendships and no real way to fix friendships that have exceeded their sell-by date.

Public friendship fallouts hurt just as much as romantic relationship breakdowns. Untagging the photos that once featured their name hurts no less when that person is a friend who's no longer your friend. There's something so humbling about going from having your bestie featured in the background of your snaps every day to muting them online and pretending that they never existed.

Lauren Conrad's iconic dialogue about forgiving and forgetting Heidi Montag in *The Hills* rings true for each friendship breakdown. No longer holding on to the reasons we wanted to be in their lives, it's easier to move on when no one is watching. The real difficulties come when you're asked questions by online audiences you once shared thousands of snaps with. When you go from a stream of content detailing how much you 'fucking loved' that babe to lone mirror selfies and picturesque views, someone is always curious enough to ask why you're no longer in your (former) best friend's life. Adhering to the 'don't ask, don't tell' principle, you'll likely politely explain that you just happened to go your separate ways and not that you had a horrendous fallout.

Accepting that the friendship deteriorated of its own accord, I always think it courteous to leave the wronged party with a fair review by way of the words 'we just parted ways, I have nothing against them!' and rating their entire performance on their metaphorical internet profile instead of rating their wrongs at the butt end of their highlight reel. It's better to pretend the split was amicable, even if it wasn't, and to distance yourselves from any wrongdoings – rather than detail the ways in which one of the two of you took things one step too far.

Unwriting old friends from new stories is tough. As with relationships that were sprawled all over your feed, the very sight of them can fill you with dread. You wonder who they might be kiki-ing with, and anxiously worry about whether or not they might've shared your most intimate and personal stories with the new friends they found to replace you. A nail in the coffin of a deadened friendship, you're never truly over this split as you're regularly reminded of the fact that they were the one to always shoot you at your best angle.

Sometimes I wish I could have weeded out the bad eggs early on to avoid any real heartbreak, but I've always been terrible at figuring out new people's real intentions. While my mother and grandmother developed their 'bad seed' radar pretty early on, mine is still in the development stage and under review until its roll-out. Unable to spot truly rotten eggs, my suspicion seems to only stretch to potential romantic partners. Avoiding catastrophic tales of heartbreak, my brain knows better than to send us back out to the battlefield when ill-prepared. We are, however, eager to get out there and start new friendships reminiscent of bathroom encounters on a drunken Saturday night. Creating new partnerships that encompass the same taste in music, wine and TV shows is often an enthralling experience, but in this hellscape known as the honeymoon phase, I'm completely blinded to new pals waving red flags such as dishing excitedly about their other friends or distancing themselves once they finally find a romantic partner.

I've always been someone who is particularly closed off to men and romantic interactions, but I'm almost scarily open with new friends. I take pride in being emotionally slutty and sharing every thought, relationship woe, win and meme, while simply basking in the early moments of bliss. I often reveal too much too soon and immediately regret it. Perhaps this is my own red flag, but in understanding and acknowledging this, maybe it's more of a pinkish hue. A flytrap for dysfunctional friendships, adult-me is learning not to divest private and intimate details without first vetting the pro-bono therapist. But I guess it doesn't hurt to have just one more life lesson on my list of 5,000.

Friends for a reason. Friends for a season. Friends for life.

—Mama Rae

My mother's wise words replay in my head when I consider the many reasons fresh friendships go sour. Not without fault, I'm old enough (and ugly enough) to admit how my wrongdoings may have contributed to the car crash called the end of a friendship, and I often use those teachings in the next encounter.

I've come to see the beauty in these words, and have applied them to all situations since. In my own 'here's to friendship' moments – like the one made famous by Millie Mackintosh, Hugo Taylor and Rosie Fortescue of *Made in Chelsea* – I raise a glass and move swiftly on, knowing that there isn't much more I could have done to salvage the dead-end relationship. The friendship breakdown of Millie Mackintosh and Rosie Fortescue was an astonishing example of how quickly betrayal can deteriorate a friendship. Although it involved a cheating scandal, it helped me to navigate confrontational situations like this in my own life with a hearty 'fuck it' attitude. Often wanting to avoid controversy, as it makes me both nauseous and anxious, this scene acted as an example of what *not* to do.

WELL, WHY DON'T YOU JUST MAKE SOME NEW FRIENDS THEN?

Manoeuvring your way through new friendships proves to be quite the difficulty in adulthood. While we may have struggled to make friends in nursery, middle and primary school, we hadn't yet experienced rejection and so were more open to being beaten with the friendship stick. Navigating how to approach new beings, although confusing and a little difficult at first, was just as new to us as learning to butter toast on our own for the first time. Today we know better than to be eager to start new friendships, for fear of being labelled a 'beg'. Making friends might just be the most stressful task in adulthood, and this is simply due to the fact that everyone is already settled in their lives, often with new homes, children and partners. At our age, it seems like everyone is comfortable, and this makes them not as open to forming new friendships or opening up their close-knit circles to new parties, which is completely understandable. My cousin Oliver often pokes me about bringing new people into our family circle, because while I'm naïve in these new relationships, he sees from the jump if they won't work in the long run.

Terrified of being the next group-chat topic, we bare our fangs and instead keep to the calm waters we're used to. Sticking to the status quo à la *High School Musical*, there's a strange fear that prevents us from being vulnerable enough to open up in new spaces, all too burdened by past interactions in friendSHITS with raging red flags. The mob mentality of exiling parties they've decided exclusively to dislike also plays its part, as you're never comfortable enough to fully be yourself for fear of being cast out of Pride Rock like Kovu in the second instalment of *The Lion King*. Waiting your turn for a social media clan to collectively dislike everything about you is not dissimilar to knowing you're about to be bullied on the school grounds.

Experiencing bullying from my school peers at a Myspace level was like child's play compared to the bullying displayed in collectives on social media today. Looking funnily at those who choose to think for themselves and make their own informed decisions, we've not learned much from our formative years, and nor have we learned from the memory of what it means to be the person on the receiving end of this mistreatment. This fear of being the outlier is one of many things discouraging us from creating new and fun adult friendships. That fear of becoming an outcast keeps us from even wanting to be involved in the first place – well, it does for me at least.

TV has always acted as my guide for navigating through life, sad as it may seem. A socially awkward kid who shone brightest within solid friendships, watching comedy series aided my inability to speak to new people and only added to my fear of making real lifelong friends. It was through Carrie's failure to be a good friend in *SATC* that I became more aware of the people in my life whom I loved dearly but who did little for me outside of aesthetics. These figures often appeared self-centred, but with sprinklings of 'oh, and how are you?' – and so, more and more, I weeded out the new Carries in my life who cared only for their well-being and ignored mine. Likely the world's worst TV friend, Carrie's onscreen example helped to determine the friends of mine who mirrored many of her behaviours and so I vetted all new friends via the Carrie Bradshaw test. Were they more invested in romantic relationships than the needs of their friends? Could they perhaps only spark conversations about themselves? Were they selfish or irresponsible with money? All of her attributes helped me to see what not to accept in platonic relationships. Assessing relationships that are bad for me via the Carrie Bradshaw algorithm has served me well.

As an advocate of 'stay far away from me, you don't want the literary smoke', I can say I'm definitely someone who knows when they like someone and when they really do not, which doesn't serve me well in creating shiny new comradery. Unsure of how to hide my very obvious facial expressions when displeased, I end up in a number of awkward situations whereby I'm expected to wear a metaphorical mask. Networking (seen as my own personal hell) is where I struggle most, as I'm prone to crumble in situations where I'm uncomfortable and unable to hide that discomfort. This means I struggle in new interactions that require me to speak on anything of substance beyond meme references and the latest media scandal. While I know many people benefit from networking, I myself only see the give-take interactions – and as someone with not much to give, the advantages of the concept escape me.

While many of my close friends may think they're in my life by happenstance, it's actually by way of initiation. Each of my very best friends, bar my cousin, was put in my life because of strategy. Whether it was Clare, whose computer screen I stalked for an opportune moment to strike up pointless conversation, or Vicki – who, sure, would technically be headed to the same university as me anyway, but whom I forced friendship upon on Twitter – this was all part of my long-game strategy to make them my lifelong friends. These friendships, truly very dear to me, are the very reason I struggle to conceptualise new and genuine connections – while these friendships were crafted, the only calculation was wanting to be their friend with no added tax, but this same approach doesn't work in the present day.

A tale of my life if I were a Caucasian woman, *Sex and the City* acted as a guide to what to look out for and how to treat friendships through different stages in adulthood. Through Charlotte's famed quote about placing emphasis on the importance of finding soulmates in your friends rather than through romantic encounters, and Samantha's perfect judgement-free interactions with the girls, I learned how to better navigate these kinds of relationships. Terrified of allowing new people in for fear of the potential destruction in my otherwise mundane life, these examples courtesy of *SATC* are ones that truly stick with me. I think we're all deserving of a friend like Samantha, and would argue that her being cut from the reboot feels a lot like the mob mentality displayed on social media when it chooses its latest outcast.

SHOOTING YA SHOT AND GETTING SHOT DOWN

I've come to realise that aimlessly shooting your shot at an MCM or WCW is something you must experience at least once in your life, and this is simply because it's incredibly humbling. I was once told that you should strive to shoot your shot even if the ball comes hurtling back at your head, which it often does, because it's much like ball practice: how will you improve and succeed with no experience? Had I not asked my Year 5 crush to be my boyfriend via the house phone, I may not have lost my virginity later on in life. Over time, and with a thousand near misses, a couple of slam dunks and the occasional facepalm moment, my confidence in wooing members of the opposite sex has only grown stronger.

What having the confidence to cold-call my crush in primary school meant was that I was never fearful of walking up to beautiful men in bars and simply saying hello when I was older. Ms Winehouse once jazzily sang about seizing the opportune moment to move on a guy on a night out, on her hit 'Know You Now', and studying these lyrics at fifteen meant I took them to heart when I was old enough to frequent local bars. This is not to say that I 'invented' shooting your shot, but I'm absolutely certain that I was doing it long before my peers. Texting *So . . . do u lyk me? Heh* was an early introduction to throwing hoops in the quest for love, and I was relentless at it.

Somewhere in the prepubescent era, I found the courage to ask the important questions, the questions that mattered. Though some might liken it to confidence, it's nothing of the sort. It's merely an inability to shut one's mouth when asking the things one probably shouldn't ask. Asking the questions that inconvenienced my mother on her days off meant that I was happy to do the same to friends and potential lovers because of a lack of shame.

As a primary schooler, my evenings were frequently spent imagining the many ways I could get my anonymous arty love notes into the colourful trays of my crush(es), which required an entire operation. Whispering secrets directly into the whorls of classmates' ears meant that we could relay a message of fancying someone throughout the classroom, to gauge the interest of the other party.

The glow-up from buck-toothed preteen to lover of System Of A Down and side-swoop hairstyles was one that even I wasn't prepared for. With this first evolution into kinda-sorta cute, it became easier to tell individuals that their faces weren't wholly terrible and that I, an inexperienced tween, would eventually like to suck face with said face. College days were spent exercising my flirtation skills and practising on anyone even remotely attractive, in the hopes of adding boys to my dating tally. It was all part of the process of honing my skills, and while many of these attempts were flat-out failures, they each taught me where I'd be in the premier league when I moved to men.

Recently, I slid into someone's DMs. I hate to be one of those 'usually I don't do this, uh' intros to a smooth R&B track, but admittedly it's my favourite once-a-year activity. As unsmooth and uncrisp as a one-week-old cucumber, I find it easier to admit I have little to no game than to embarrass myself via DM, which is my sole reason for rarely doing it.

Imagine my horror when discovering that the incredibly handsome man whose face I pictured next to mine on a couple's holiday to the Caribbean was five years my junior. Immediately grossed out by the fact I'd entered a man's online sphere, attempted to woo him and failed to ask the most important question up front, I'm here to share my unmitigated failure. A little rusty in the game, like Rusty Rust-eze from *Cars*, it makes sense why I'd have misplaced my list of first-date questions – you know, 'Do you go to therapy?' 'When did you last get tested?' 'Have you any childhood trauma?' Age. Who doesn't ask for an age?! It's evident that I was more terrified of the shot landing than any of the details that followed – be that criminal records, lingering ex-partners, or whether or not our ages matched.

I tend not to shoot my shot unless I really, truly am moved. Because more often than not, the face is fantastic while the humour is lacking, which means a wasted effort. In my heyday, with confidence in my demeanour, I greatly enjoyed telling handsome men I enjoyed their face. However, with my now moving from the 18–24 to the 25–34 box, I shudder when considering the dating world. Until now, I never considered that age would be a blocker, because I foolishly assumed everyone was just my age. With my peers and I all growing at the same speed, I thought we'd all reach the same milestone of thirty on the same date at 00.00.

Though age has of course been a factor in my life on many occasions. We only have to look as far as my short-lived holiday romance on a family trip to Barbados. At nineteen I met someone considerably older, and when we returned home, we both quickly realised how far removed we were from one another's lives.

To put it into context, my brief holiday romance was ready to buy his first home while I was still figuring out how to readjust to living with my parents – if only temporarily – when home from university over the summer. He was six foot four with a stunning smile and rocking the tallest high-top fade I'd ever seen, and I waited patiently for the tall, handsome man to notice me posing in the sun on Brownes Beach, which he of course never did. His friends left with him in tow, each covered in sand and with a towel slung over their shoulders, and I made peace with the fact that I'd probably never see another man that hot in my life. That was until later that night, when my stepdad somehow persuaded the two eldest members of the kiddie crew (my sister and I) to come to an evening concert in the park with my uncle. The rules from my stepdad were simple:

1. We drive there together as a group.

2. We separate as soon as we arrive.

3. We leave together as a group.

Embarrassed by his daughters' presence, my stepdad quickly applied Rule No. 2 and bolted from our view with my uncle. Purchasing a bottle of Mount Gay Rum with our allocated vacation pocket money, we took this as our green light to get absolutely fucked. Hopping around the soca event with little balance and all of the confidence, I spotted him – my dream man from the beach. With more than enough courage mixed into my drinks, I scuttled over to this handsome stranger and told him quite frankly that I liked his face. We discovered that we lived in the same area in London and joked that it must have been fate, because why else would we have met in the middle of Barbados? After one too many shots of brown liquor we locked lips and my parent-free evening felt as though it was just beginning. My friends aptly called it 'pulling a Lauren', as I was not averse to kissing handsome strangers on a night out once I'd had a few.

He and I exchanged numbers and, once reunited with the adults, my family and I headed home. While everyone was fighting sleep, I smiled ear to ear knowing that my holiday crush crushed on me right back. The next morning, he texted me and I squealed, as he was asking if he could take me on a *real* date, and I of course accepted. But there was one minor snag: I wasn't *technically* allowed to go out alone, and had to be accompanied by my older sister. Though she rolled her eyes, she accepted the task, and while he and

I sipped cocktails at a bar in St Lawrence Gap, she danced the night away with pals at a club nearby.

As with my slide into the DMs, I forgot to ask for an age. Having just completed my second year of university, my career was weekends at Wembley Stadium, while he had an actual career. The first thorn in our holiday romance mirage. When he told me he worked for Google, I giggled because my immaturity led me to believe it was computers and robots that were behind this mysterious search engine. I consider this snag number two. Despite being attracted to each other, the very large maturity gap began to make me uncomfortable as I realised that I was almost infantile in comparison.

This vast difference between the two of us opened my eyes to my dating preferences in age, as I'd have sooner died than succumbed to a small 'lol' via text from an older man as it's typically their form of communication. Not just a lost-in-translation communication, this experience left me cold about dating anyone significantly my senior, out of fear they may regard me childish or feel misunderstood.

Some years later, with my embarrassing life occurrences stacking up like the gold in the sandcastle in Disney's *Aladdin,* I was curious about branching out of my comfort zone and the preferred age brackets detailed on my Bumble and Tinder profiles. In an episode of *SATC* where Carrie dates a significantly older man, her *Vogue* editor Enid discusses the problem with dating age-appropriate men – saying that her dating pool is significantly smaller than Carrie's due to her older age. The scene reminds me a lot of approaching thirty. With fewer and fewer single parties out there, Enid's words strike a chord.

Love Is Blind's Jessica, who made it her mission to detail her and her chosen partners' ages constantly on the show, is a prime example of what it would mean for me to date below my age bracket. While the series indicated that they could maybe be perfect for one another, Jessica could not let go of this issue.

Still, after making the huge error of not asking his age in my flawed attempt at shooting my shot, I began googling women with younger partners and wondering if perhaps I could be one of those hot older women. In two minds about whether to be a MILF without the kids, I found myself fantasising about all the couples with younger partners who made it work and looked great in their side-by-side red carpet photo ops. Then the thought of being judged washed over me, and even looking at the beautiful smiling faces of Gabrielle Union and Dwyane Wade I struggled to come to terms with the concept of always being the older one. While I was trying to figure out a way to potentially make this misfired shot work, the realisation soon hit me that I would always be stressing about the age gap, and I reminded myself of the brief holiday encounter that had failed at the first hurdle because of age when I was nineteen. Worrying about what my most judgemental peers might think and about having to disclose my partner's age when asked, I knew that I would struggle beyond the concept of 'we're both just peng and having fun'. I was unable to distance myself from the idea that I might be doing something wrong if I succumbed to dating men significantly younger than me, even though the age gap of this plucky new individual would still of course be within reason.

OH WAIT . . . IS THIS A DATE-DATE?

At twenty-six, recently single after John Doe 2 and still unable to detect relationship social cues, my relationship radar needed some fine-tuning. Freelancing alongside my full-time job, I met a guy. His Jil Sander accessories accented his slim frame, and I audibly said 'rah' as he politely brushed past me in the lift. This would be the very beginning of a story I still don't quite understand and have yet to fit into my list of 'yeah . . . maybe don't do that again'.

Despite the encounter with this handsome individual lasting a mere five seconds, I was quickly located on social media in full romantic-comedy fashion. With just my first name, the incredibly handsome stranger was able to find me via a handle that did not even contain my name. Okay, no, that's just low-key creepy. But he was hot.

Bribed with the possibility of a lunch date, I reluctantly returned to my freelance gig faced with a new challenge outside of the work I was tasked with. Unable to decipher whether this lunch date was friendly or romantic, I replayed what Carrie said when she first began dating Aidan Shaw where she questioned whether he was more of a boyfriend, or a friend.

Surely the notion that he had scoured the internet in search of my @ should have been enough for me to believe someone had a genuine interest in me, but instead I spent the entirety of the lunch with questions swirling around in my brain. Dining on fine Italian cuisine, I wavered between trying to look cute while necking pasta and not giving a fuck because it might *not* be a date anyway . . . right? Every time I looked up from my five-star meal, I was met with his fucking beautiful face and came up with a new conclusion. He was far too hot for me. (Friend.) Perhaps I deserve a hot boy-friend?! (Romantic.) Despite the meal being comped by my new friend (?), our friendship (?) fizzled and we soon became Instagram pen pals – which is how I like to refer to the people who react to my posts every now and then. When we went on our second date two years later, I was told that the lunch encounter I'd struggled to decipher was in fact the first date.

Misunderstanding and navigating intentions via hints will never make logical sense to me and my dense ill-equipped dating brain. As someone who has always spoken her mind even when the world tells her it's time to shut the F up, I respond only to being told at length of someone's interest. This way I'm able to develop the ick that comes with the abhorrent thought of a relationship with intimacy.

Netflix's *Bridgerton*, which became an overnight sensation due to its Georgian sex scenes and devilishly handsome main character, was like the pages of my diary when I was eighteen come to life, minus all the raucous caterwauling. Quaint stares and banter with a best friend is part of the story of my life, and arguably my favourite chapter. At a young age, men not admitting to liking me or saying that they were actually interested – with their mouths along with their actions – led me to believe we were all just flirting with one another for the lols.

Taking the 'my hand is up for grabs to other potential suitors and you're holding up the line, sir' approach, *Bridgerton*'s Daphne is naturally enamoured with the Duke, but still seeking out other options because he refuses to admit he's into her – a concept dear to my heart. Because why should a beautiful young woman wait for the bare minimum when there are men who would outright declare their love for her from the rooftops? Waste not, want not, and time waits for no man. Seeking potential suitors in a rigorous 1800s version of the Tinder dating game, Daphne Bridgerton seeks affection from men who dote on her, while also pining for the love of her life due to his inability to speak up and claim her for his own. It's not unlike my dating experience today.

LOVE IN TRANSLATION

Dating as a foreigner working abroad is not unlike a sordid holiday romance – and, much like the participants on *Love Island*, we 'couple up' with anyone we feel an instant connection with because of its scarcity. I learned this lesson quite quickly when I up and moved to Munich, Germany.

Awkward dates aside, there is always a 1 in 1,000 chance of experiencing a good first, second or third date. Partially due to the fact that I frequently date via the friends-turned-lovers method, and feel uncomfortable in default *love* settings without the assistance of a glass of red.

With a number of experiences under my belt now, I can express that dating abroad has a certain allure and fun to it that dating at a local restaurant does not have. This includes brief holiday romances, datecations – and yes, even the less commonly known baecation. Exploring fresh terrain with someone you're kind of into is nothing short of exciting, and their generosity, seen in new countries, is something that gets the metaphorical motor running. In these circumstances, we're able to experience one another at full capacity, either resulting in the ick or full-blown obsession.

However, my brief Munich encounters were anything but a fairy tale, unless of course it was a fairy tale filled with fuckboys, mansplainers and the sci-fi trope where there's a big red button you're told not to press – in this case the block button. While I'm definitely grateful for these experiences, they were just that for me: experiences.

Before moving, I was privy to a datecation that saw me taken to Nice, France. My first dating experience abroad was another of those situations where I did not realise it was doused with the gasoline of romance. Once again unable to see someone's interest in me, despite the trip being all-expenses-paid, I went in with an open mind in terms of growing the friendship, though this already strong friendship soon blossomed into the 'other' category. Flirting with the 'it's complicated' option seen only on Facebook, this introduction to dating abroad was exciting, fresh and new. *Could real first dates abroad be the secret to successful new relationships?* Introducing myself to the concept of saying 'yes' now and thinking it through later, this new-age dating was exciting to me.

Then there are those dating experiences abroad that offer you the ick earlier than you expected. Getting to grips with someone's behaviour in general is an experience, but doing it in a situation where you're stuck together for an extended period of time is quite another. From passing comments to bathroom habits, you're subjected to each of the red flags you'd usually only be privy to at the very last hurdle before making it to an official relationship – which I guess is a blessing in disguise?

No, I didn't block you, but here's why I should have . . . As with many things that happen in my life, dating in Germany started off as a joke while blindly drunk from Prosecco. Beginning innocently enough, a friend and I downloaded both Bumble and Tinder and swiped right on a plethora of okay-looking guys. Was I finally ready to allow a man I didn't understand to make me laugh? Perhaps. Immediately, there were three men that caught my attention when I glanced at my glaringly bright iPhone screen. The morning after the night before felt like a hangover in more ways than one, as I began to feel anxious about the probability of people I knew IRL seeing my profile on one of the two apps.

Much like *Shrek*'s poignant scene with Lord Farquaad's potential marriage conquests, I began my dating diary with three eligible bachelors. Though, instead of a talking mirror, I selected my potential dates by way of dating apps on my smartphone. Bachelor No. 1 was cute and didn't live in Munich, but was a frequent visitor from Hamburg. Bachelor No. 2 smoked weed, was tall and had an adorable dog. Bachelor No. 3 was just plain hot. Matching with these men in this exact order, the thrill of 'You've got a new match!' messages was short-lived and I do wish I'd cottoned on to the fact that sometimes bad things happen in threes.

My first attempt at dating in Germany was a complete and utter bust. Bachelor No.1 attempted to squeeze our debut date in with his fifty-five other plans, which meant his earlier dinner with friends ran long – two hours long, to be exact. Glammed up and nervous about my first encounter with a man in well over nine months, my Fenty Beauty Gloss Bomb began to lose its sheen and my under-eye concealer started to dry. I was well past the sell-by date of make-up magic – that two-hour window where my make-up still looked flawless from all angles.

Via WhatsApp, my prospective date sent multiple messages about being another twenty minutes behind, but by that point I was completely over it. I untied my braids from the tension hair-style I'd put them up in, and washed my face. Finally done with his dinner at 10.30 p.m., Bachelor No.1 texted that he was ready to meet and I should send him a location, a suggestion I politely declined. His outrage and my reluctance to leave my flat two hours after the proposed date saw some 20+ messages detailing why I was a bitch for standing him up and that my looks would only get me so far in life. Our flailing encounter ended there, and I put the experience down to just not being ready for such a stark transition from no dates to utterly deranged men who could actually kill me given the chance. It was time to try again . . . right?

Some days later, Bachelor No. 2 messaged me after some witty repartee back and forth. He was cute, tall and obsessed with his dog, all traits I thought to be green flags. He proposed that we finally hang out in the real world as he wanted to see my smile in person. Fair. I didn't, as Cardi B so eloquently puts it, get a bag and correct my smile for no reason. So, dragging one of my colleagues along for the ride, I ventured out on my first Bumble date in Germany. My friend and colleague Holly was the perfect fifth wheel to an event I was certain I'd leave come 9 p.m.

Heading out for an Aperol Spritz, I held my breath when I first saw him standing and gesturing me over. 'Oh fuck, he's hot,' I said as Holly nodded in agreement. We walked over to the spot he had saved and greeted his friends. So there we were with a couple, Bachelor No. 2, Holly, the dog and myself – one big, happy family.

Unheard of for many of my first dates, this went swimmingly. We all got along and there was clearly an attraction between us. I felt a sense of ease that my first actual date with someone abroad had gone well, and patted myself on the back for having gone through with it. The date went on until after midnight, and he graciously offered to drive me home where we had our first kiss. *Okay*, I thought to myself. *Dating here isn't* that *shitty*. Keen to see me again, he proposed a few days when we could potentially hang, and I agreed.

ONE NEW MESSAGE

Hey! Wanna come to Austria with me on my business trip?

My initial thought was to Print Screen and share with my friends before responding. *Should I go?????? I don't know if I should go.* Weighing up the pros and cons of this potential datecation, at first I politely declined, putting my deadlines and safety at the forefront, until I came to my senses. Or lack thereof, in this case. I was told to pack for dinner, the spa and several walks around Kitzbühel between his meetings. Three days later, we set off on what I thought would be a romantic-comedy-esque road trip.

We got along like a house on fire, and I loved how comfortable I was around him. Then the red flags started showing themselves about two hours into the three-hour car journey when he prefaced a question with 'Is it racist if . . . ?' My heart dropped. *Fuck my life*, I thought, *you couldn't have asked this back in Munich so I could get up and go home?!* I, of course, detailed the reasons why, whatever the question is, beginning a sentence with that statement means what's

133

to follow is likely racist. It's the same as saying 'I'm not trying to be rude but . . .' and then following it with a very rude sentiment. We clashed, as his ignorance meant that he couldn't see things from the other side, and it turned into a series of uncomfortable political debates about race and the discomfort of being the only black person in predominantly white spaces – particularly the one we were in. With one or two comebacks and a chuckle here and there, the datecation was pretty unsalvageable and I waited tirelessly for my eventual ride back to Munich. The following morning, after a day spent apart or nodding at one another and responding with one- or two-word answers, we drove back in silence. I guess we'd sort of made a silent pact to just never hang out again, as he unfollowed me on Instagram and that was the end of that weird whirlwind love affair.

Upon returning from one of the worst dating experiences of my life, I thought, *Fuck it! Why not one more?* Third time's the charm and all that. Bachelor No. 3 was the hot one who I'd had my eye on from the very beginning, so I figured that by the process of elimination he was the chosen one. No. 3 must have heard my calls for instant gratification, as he contacted me about a drink the moment I returned from my hellish overnight stay. *Should I wash the taste of a bad date out of my mouth with fresh meat?* I accepted, though I had no intention of actually attending, and instead had a girls' night with Teresa, a close friend, where I complained about the kinds of men attracted to me.

The date wasn't to be, and he apologised for not following up though it was technically a mutual fault. He proposed that I watch the footie with him and his flatmate, and to add to my long string of YOLO events, I said yes, restoring some self-confidence that it wasn't me, it was them. When I arrived, I wondered if perhaps this was where I was being lured to my death, because what the fuck was I doing going to a stranger's house for the first hang-out? I immediately texted three friends with a live location, and proceeded with caution.

As it turned out, it was just the refreshing non-date I needed to get over the events of the nights before. My faith in men was restored, albeit slightly, as I felt somewhat attractive and led with my finest personality traits: my taste in music + humour. Our bond was an interesting one, as he taught me German words and phrases in exchange for UK slang. But the illusion of the perfect potential partner soon shattered the moment I left. We arranged to hang again at some point, and it just never happened. One morning I woke to a message that read, *Why did you block me on WhatsApp???* as I looked at my Instagram DMs befuddled before even indulging in my morning coffee.

Things only got weirder as I explained that I hadn't actually blocked him and had no clue what he was going on about. I had, after all, planned to see him the following day and was quite giddy about the prospect of this second encounter. However, his radio silence following my explanation led me to believe he must have been too embarrassed to respond. Either that, or this was the weirdest way to get out of a second date – second only to Carrie's breakup Post-it note from Jack Berger. The bizarre encounter left me even more confused than I am when I overhear my neighbours arguing outside my flat. And so I concluded that my taste in men was fucking weird and perhaps this was just the universe's way of screaming 'YOU STILL *CAN'T* DO IT' while I attempted dating's version of a couch-to-5K.

The Writer on her Crumbling Bank Balance

Chapter 4: The Writer On Her Crumbling Bank Balance

Hello, Bank Balance, ca-can I talk to you for a minute?
It's me, your unexpected overdraft, plus the added charges
for not having paid said unexpected overdraft.

No one said that being a writer would be easy, and rightly so. Between the flawed invoice payment system, my inability to chase said invoices and the anxiety during moments of pitch rejection, writing frequently feels like a devil's picnic. What I'm saying here is that a lot of the time it feels like falling seven times and just staying down on the eighth.

Despite an intense love of the written word, I'm regularly plagued by the knowledge that it will *probably* never fund the million-dollar home I hope to acquire in the near future, and it's even less likely to help me rent a yacht for my next big birthday. In the wise words of YouTuber Nella Rose, I just want to shake my ass on a yacht, and being a failed writer just doesn't feel like it'll help me to achieve this dream. When times are tough, which is more often than not, I think of packing it in, changing my identity entirely and jetting off to the Caribbean for a simpler life. Truth be told, writers – and I'm massively generalising here, soz – often envision themselves in sunnier settings, writing on expensive laptops with a to-die-for view, and television is probably to blame for this seemingly unachievable dream. Thanks a lot (Carrie) Bradshaw and (Betty) Suarez.

Thoughts of quitting and moving on to something far more lucrative often haunt me, and I'm sure it's the same with many of us twenty-somethings. Sure, I might give up more often than Tyra Banks recounts the times Naomi Campbell was mean to her, but I always end up back in love with writing. It seems to have the same gravitational pull as one's lady parts do when they're falling for a certain person. In other words: blinding stupidity.

Case in point, here I am writing a book. Wait, can you say that? Can you talk about writing a book . . . in a book? It may be too meta, but the point is, writing is the unhealthiest relationship I've ever had, and that includes the ones where I pined after someone and made a fool of myself. Of which there have been plenty. Truth be told, I've been a complete and utter donkey swaddle for many men in my past – but none of those situations are even the slightest bit comparable to the written word and me. No, seriously – and while I know my best friends are likely looking up from this chapter, pursing their lips and following it up with a '*Que?*' – I assure you this is so. Writing can make me look more of a fool than any man ever could. Every other day, I declare that I'm over it and that I'll move on to something new like, I dunno, coal mining or spearfishing. But I always go right back and feel ever more foolish each time I do, with the hope that maybe this will be the one that gets me a follow-up book deal or a coveted position at *Elle*.

IF ONLY Ls COULD BE USED AS CURRENCY

I suspect you don't quite know what taking an L is like until you've been rejected by more jobs than men. Ls (or losses as they're also known) are not unfamiliar to me, as I've experienced a series of them since my conception in the early 1990s. I'm talking about the kind of Ls you received in your teenhood, when a cluster of spots set up camp on your greasy forehead and distract from your slicked-down edges or blunt-cut fringe; the kinds of Ls that were followed by out-loud laughter. Much of that laughter still lives with me today, and seeing the funny side is pretty much the only way I can deal with being a failed writer.

At school, and using my allotted £10 a week, I learned quite quickly that there was an art to being broke. I was an entrepreneur, I guess. From an early age, I familiarised myself with being – from a celebrity's standpoint – poor. With that £10, I'd spend £7.50 on a five-day pass (what kids in the 2000s used to talk to their potential baes all night, all morning and all day), and would use the remaining £2.50 for lunch . . . for the entire week. Sure, it was technically my own fault and I didn't really *need* a five-day pass, but through this I was taught the art of hustling – or rather scrounging throughout the week. Ever fearful of going back to my mother for more pocket money, and keen to avoid the 'value of money' speech, I used every trick in the book to make sure my lunches were the cheapest, most filling and, often, free.

Though I hate to admit it, my crumbling bank balance isn't limited to adulthood and its barrage of unpaid invoices; I've actually been pretty broke my whole life. Self-inflicted brokeness, but brokeness nonetheless. Using the last of my pennies, I was teaching myself that lacking money wasn't the end of the world, though it certainly seems that way in the present day due to my growing interest in designer purses and bottomless brunches. With prices being slightly different at that time (largely because 11–15 Oyster cards were a thing, making travel an absolute doddle), the extent of my struggles was self-inflicted.

Yet, beyond the all-time minimum costs of being a high-school student, my progressing puberty meant that I'd soon be moving on to new realms of being broke, and then came my college days. If you didn't have access to EMA (Education Maintenance Allowance), from a college student's standpoint you were poor. Used as leverage to let the other kids know that you were £15–30 richer than them, EMA was granted to students who showed up to college on time. Not qualifying for this additional income, I had a growing disdain for being punctual as I wasn't getting paid for it, and there was no real incentive to show up or be on time past the first few weeks of college. Tired of watching my peers squander their punctuality earnings on the latest creps at JD Sports, I instead turned my efforts to eventually finding a shitty part-time job so that I had something else to impress the boys I fancied.

Additional maintenance grants at university followed the same principle, with richer students lording their additional three-grand grants over those of us who were subject to the poor-student life. For us mere paupers who only had enough to cover the surging costs of student rent, ample cups of tea were used to suppress hunger until the next big meal. My broke meal of choice felt a long way from the Lurpak-buttered toast I had when living at home. I realised that Lurpak was a privilege, and I downgraded to ketchup without a brand name and butter of the same ilk. At this stage in my life, I was given just a taste of the struggles faced as a *real* grown-up and was forced to sit mock exams for adulthood, which I failed terribly. This is when I learned that money was a pretty big deal, and having to find money to pay for bills and shit is a struggle that follows me today. My goodness, I hate it here sometimes.

FIGURE IT OUT M8, AND FAST!

It's insane to think about the pressures placed on sixteen-year-olds to start thinking about their adult careers. When you remember how you were incapable of even selecting the correct button on the till at your first part-time job, it's crazy to think that we were forced to decide our entire futures based on the subjects we chose at A-level and/or BTEC.

With a number of short-term retail jobs under my belt, the worst of the bunch was the one full week I spent working at a shop that I still refuse to ever use due to mistreatment. It was the first time I'd ever had a black boss, outside of the quick jobs my stepdad afforded me, and I was excited to work under someone who looked like me by way of race – only he wasn't like me at all. Quite the opposite, actually. Similar to the black teachers I had at high school who seemed to me to work me twice as hard so as to 'toughen me up for the real world', his method of training on-the-go felt more like bullying than a helping hand.

On my first day, I was placed on the till without any training on how to use this jazzy new piece of equipment that looked like the controls of an alien spaceship to me. He stood back and watched me struggle, before pulling me aside and explaining that it was unacceptable to work to this standard. Watching the other new starters try in the same way and yet be afforded courtesy, my anxiety worsened as I tried to understand why I was being treated differently when we were making the exact same mistakes. At the end of my first and only week at this company, and after cashing up my till after a day spent swallowing my tears, my manager pulled me aside to relay some bad news. 'Unfortunately,' he began, 'we're going to have to let you go. Your till has come up short, which proves that you've been stealing from it.' I fought the urge to cry in the backroom. Me? Steal? From a company I adored and had access to a discount from? It just wasn't true. I tried to fight the accusation, but his stern look suggested it had very little to do with the missing pennies and everything to do with the fact that he just didn't want me working there.

Gathering my belongings and the shoes I'd bought to wear on my shift with my discount, I left the store filled with shame, brushing past my now ex-colleagues as they all said, 'See ya tomorrow, Lauren!' I was entirely too ashamed to admit that I would likely never see them again. I saved my tears for the second train home, living in fear that one of my colleagues would see me on the first train and ask what was wrong. That day, I learned that sharing the same race does not make you allies.

Finding a viable career path in life was a struggle in itself, but I had the added pressure of family members who made it their mission to remind me how important this decision was for my future. It was all well and good having a part-time job, but once those contracts came to a close, there was always the anxiety-inducing question 'What are you planning to do next?' Even now, a grown-up (lol) with her own bills and more than one debit card with my name on it, I still do not know the answer. Instead, I look to my idols Tracee Ellis Ross and Gabrielle Union as examples of who I hope to be when I grow up. But like *grow up* grow up – past the beta stage of whatever faux-adult timeline I'm in right now.

Had I known the impact my decisions at GCSE level would have, perhaps I'd have aimed for a career in coding and put my Myspace skills to use. Instead, I traded in my coding knowledge for Facebook albums and underage drinking memories in the park with friends that I wish we could bury deep beneath the internet-sphere.

Not yet understanding how much our decisions in our teenage years would greatly affect our adult years, we were keen to explore subjects like Art, much to our parents' dismay. Suggesting we select one of the STEM subjects we had little to no interest in, they subtly pushed us in the direction of subjects that would better our understanding of the real adult world. With no clue what the fuck I wanted to do with my life after high school, I behaved like the plastic bag in Katy Perry's hit 'Firework'. Flying on the wind and very easily swayed, I cared little for my education once I was free from the bullying I experienced in my final years at school. If it were up to me, I'd have likely bagged myself a minimum-wage job and complained about it until the age I am now. Though I guess not that much would be different.

Torn between not wanting to disappoint my mother and grandmother and not giving a shit about further education affecting my upcoming adult years, I had the urge to explore my options. Still, adhering to the wishes of my parents, I completed a number of different college applications, selecting two of the 'bait' colleges I'd heard of in passing from friends.

Having always been obsessed with English and correcting people's homework, I considered a combination course of English Literature and Performing Arts. Ever the class clown, I thought it perfect for me, as I would get to act – and act a fool – all day during lessons. That was until I realised that this particular course would require an audition for the Performing Arts portion of the course. While sure, I was fantastic at making an ass of myself unprovoked, I was less successful doing this on command, and soon this would prove to be a problem. I was called in for an audition and some form of written work some days later. I absolutely floored the written task. This was of course years before I began wrecking my brain cells with constant sips of red wine, and I was cleverer than a whip. The day my audition arrived, I walked the halls of what I hoped would be my new stomping grounds, and I was numb with fear. Shaking on my way up the stairs, I knew I was about to completely tank the audition part of the interview process.

He asked me what my hopes, ambitions and dreams were, which was easy for me because they almost all involved writing of some sort and talking about writing filled me with glee. It soon came time to pick a song to sing and a monologue to act out. I of course chose Amy Winehouse's 'You Know I'm No Good' as I had played it on repeat the entire way there, and despite my embarrassment at one or two missed words and using the phrase 'skulk T-shirt' in place of 'skull T-shirt', the interviewer seemed pretty sold. But this might have been due to my overall dedication to Winehouse, as I was rocking her signature beehive at the time. However, the monologue is where I lost his interest; I remember the lecturer's face dropping at my unsuccessful attempts to finish a full sentence without my voice cracking. Similarly to my final oral Spanish exam, I knew this audition was going to land me a Grade D and that I was *not* getting into this college. But, despite being riddled with embarrassment at the shambolic second half of the audition, I wasn't at all fussed. Instead, I was eager to get the FUCK OUT, ASAP, and go back to the drawing board – which meant repeatedly telling my mother I had no idea what I wanted to do with my life.

Despite not really wanting to study, well, anything at a collegiate level, I was frequently reminded that if I didn't do it now at age sixteen, it would cost me later. And that's not to say not going would have hindered me, but the literal cost of further education college after age eighteen is abysmal. Though I'm not sure of the price now, I remember being sickened by the knowledge that I would have had to spend money from my weekend-job paycheque to fund an education if I waited another two years. Unfair to those who've had to postpone their education for legitimate reasons, the imbalance in this time-sensitive education timeline negatively affects mature students – and young students – who haven't yet been afforded the time to figure life out.

Even now, I look back and wonder if my not knowing what to do then impacted my not knowing what to do now. With no easier plight in sight, the decisions about my future would only grow harder for me as time went on. Handling my shit at a new level, when I started university I not only had to select a subject that would impact my future, but also a subject that would impact my future at *cost*. Forking out thousands, I had to be sure of what I wanted to study, as I only really had one shot to get it right. Now that I think about it, a lot of my higher education only happened due to scaremongering tactics, because I could have just as easily become someone's sugar baby aged nineteen and been content with my role as a faux-housewife. One who doesn't cook but mans the house and looks pretty once a month or so. With my cheekbones at their peak at that time, I really missed a golden opportunity to use my youthful looks for money.

Never really knowing what I wanted to do, and being repeatedly told I had years to figure it out – but not really having that much time at all – I felt like I'd been lied to my whole entire existence. I'm still told frequently that I've got some years yet to figure it out, but that time is less and less as age catches up with me. As I sit here today, making sure my handbag doesn't touch the floor for fear of the curse of being poor, I can't help but wonder, should I have been an electrician?

Desperate to find my calling, I studied a print-based media course at college. My grandmother immediately voiced her concerns, and informed me that heading down the writer route would be a dead end, but of course I didn't listen. She was correct. I mean, every lesson at college following that conversation spoke of the 'significant decline in journalism', and every teacher hammered on about just how much print media was dying. But even with all this knowledge in my mind, I still looked to the written word as something of a saviour, thinking of it as the Jack to my Rose – when it was in fact the iceberg to my sinking ship. Completely disregarding my grandmother's words, I ploughed on towards journalism with my eyes wide shut.

Instead of aiming for the more sustainable career option of becoming an electrician, I spent many of my days at college giggling at the lads studying the trades, but in reality they had the real dish. Knowing that there was a high demand for those positions, they dove head first into a pit of cash. I suspect they likely bottled up my past giggles and could use them on me in the present day, and rightly so. Wanting to be creative, I had other plans, hoping that one day my passion would be enough to get me into the printed pages of *i-D*, solely based on the fact that I could speak poetically of my love of the written word. And though I jested at those studying electrics in my teens, it was because I strived to be doing something more than what I deemed a regular-degular job at that time. I wanted to be surrounded by like-minded people bouncing ideas off one another, similar to the meetings shown on *Ugly Betty*. The future, or so I thought, held bigger things than my little home town of Harrow. I envisioned myself at the head of a giant round table, with a flipchart purchased by my favourite intern and an array of colourful ideas.

Longing to be in a creative space is likely the cause of my descent into madness, because as a creative you pretty much have to be open to the notion that not getting where you want in your career (achievements big or small) may drive you utterly insane. Our own toughest critics, we need constant wins in order to feel like we're moving forward and on to better things. With every knock it feels as though you're being pushed right off the ladder, and with every no or 'Sorry, we can only offer peanuts and exposure', it feels like the world doesn't really need your talents. It's a nightmare rollercoaster, kids. Hands up if you relate . . .

PAY US . . . PLEASE?

The terrible thing about writing – well, *one* of the terrible things – is that although writers are in high demand, people don't *actually* want to pay them for their efforts. Not really. If you think about all the websites, magazines, adverts and smoothie labels that need copy, for example, surely there should be a high demand for copy-writers. Without copy, articles about new celebrity scandals would be like a silent movie, minus the title cards. Okay, it looks cool as fuck, but like WTF is actually taking place here? Advertisements would be more nude than the pages of *Playboy* circa '94; websites would be confusing, with everyone unsure of what fabric that fabulous co-ord is actually made from. And the sad reality is that fashion magazines likely wouldn't exist, unless you're into adoring clothes on models and it doesn't kill you dead not to know where the world's dreamiest garments are from.

With a crumbling bank balance as just one of the cons of attempting to be the next Kenya Hunt, it's likely my account cries as much as I do when an offer finally comes through. Routinely told my work is worth X when it takes the entire fucking alphabet to create, creation is as tiresome as it sounds. I mean, it only takes a couple of excruciating days to come up with a concept and build up the courage to pitch it, only to be told that the magazine doesn't quite have the budget to pay for it – which, as I'm now saying this, is a process that probably applies to the creative industry as a whole. Though there are a few publications who are happy to take you on – and the prospect of having a byline in another magazine means you often take their offer. Even if it means being paid in pennies.

For me, my first big win came in the form of my first paid article for Refinery 29. I remember so well the creative process leading up to that moment, because I was terrified that the editor would turn around and say, 'Actually, we've changed our minds, could you naff off?' And that would be it – my dreams shot to hell. Lucky for me, it came through, and was probably what led me to know my worth in the writing world. From the moment that link went up online, I made the creative decision to stop taking on roles for the exposure and instead only accept projects that paid me for my time. This was it – I was like, officially, a freelance writer. Though the work decreased, I had some confidence that I'd be paid big sometime soon. Spoiler alert: I wasn't, lol.

My life as a freelancer was incredibly short-lived. I made the decision to make that leap, but I immediately regretted it. Plagued by panic attacks as a result of a previous full-time job that I despised, every bump in the freelancer road felt like an earthquake on my solo island. At that time, and after having such a regular income for so long, I couldn't imagine not knowing when the next paycheque would come in. I was terrified, and so I sought advice from other freelancers. While some assured me that my fears were justified, others put the fear of God in me that I'd made an entirely wrong choice.

Conflicted about the decision I'd made for my life and career, I eventually caved. Starting from the bottom, hoping to work my way up, I became an intern (for free) all over again. During 2016, while I still had some freelance gigs going, they didn't pay well enough or regularly enough to keep up with my lifestyle – and by 'lifestyle', I mean shoe obsession and tireless wanderlust.

Yet, still a hopeful twenty-something, I interned at seven different places. I figured the more titles under my belt, the more likely I was to be hired, right? I transcribed interviews, assisted on layouts, and even got a few pieces of work out there, but I was less than satisfied with my career prospects. My only real desire was to make money from writing because, hello, I was good at it (kinda), plus I had pending holidays and bills to pay, and I was fed up of being terrified to look at my bank account at the end of every internship. It was time for a change, and I needed to act quickly, because my current account was screaming, 'I need some MILK!'

DID YOU KNOW YOU HAVE TO WORK . . . TO PAY THE BILLS?

I want to preface this by saying that working for a living feels a lot like the world's biggest scam. This isn't what God created Adam and Eve to do, and I'm not quite sure how her eating an apple has landed us at the forefront of capitalism some hundreds of thousands of years later. A prank played on those of us whose desire it is to spend six months at a time on a beach and frolicking with our mates, we've been forced to believe that there's some normalcy to getting up every day before 9 a.m. and working until 6 p.m. And for what? A paycheque.

I started out in the working world like so many of us do, with a (weekend?) job in retail. The only job I remember not actually minding was at House of Fraser, because it really was the beginning of my trajectory into adulting and responsibility. Looking back, I didn't love the job, but it provided me with incredible friends and a fresh new outlook on life. Though it wasn't my first job *ever*, it was my first time being an independent woman as I wasn't living at home at the time. Commuting from my shitty little flat in Leicester to London every weekend forced me to work ten times harder in every aspect of my life. That meant working hard to perfect my friendships, my university grades *and* my home life. I felt like a real-life grown-up, even with such little income. Because, realistically, £400 a month was hardly worth the hour-long commute to London and studying during said commute. But I couldn't go back to asking for hand-outs – not when I'd already started being independent and earning my own money. So I refused, and I kept that job for a lot longer than I should have, because essentially every penny I made went towards rent, food and a persistent Zara obsession as it was located opposite my place of work.

Soon enough though, it came time to move on. I was almost a graduate, and 'sales assistant at House of Fraser' just didn't scream fashion writer. So I found myself a lil ol' 9-to-5(.30), and continued my journey to adulthood. Though it wasn't yet my dream job, it was a stepping stone towards the end goal. I remember walking into HOF with my letter of resignation and feeling incredibly accomplished. Two weeks of interning at a publishing company, one job interview and a couple of missed shifts later, I was well on my way to really exploring the big city – Farringdon, to be precise. My work bestie at the time, Naomi, had said, 'I knew you weren't coming back,' the day I walked into HOF with that shoddily handwritten letter, and she was right. Once I'd had a taste of what I thought the real world was meant to be like, I couldn't bear the thought of losing my weekends anymore – not for such a petty amount of cash. This also came at a time when my bank balance frequently told me I was living well beyond my means. A broke bitch with a rich-bitch mentality, I was ready for more. I mean, we can't all sit at home and be paid rent, shoe and food money off of one column a week – and yes, that is a direct dig at Carrie.

At twenty-one and having just graduated from university, I was terrified that the world would immediately forget that I actually had a degree, and so anxiety won, and I caved and nabbed myself a shitty desk job. Shitty, because while I spent my Mondays to Fridays in a cold, desolate and grey environment, my recent-graduate pals were out day-drinking in Shoreditch and sending crude messages along the lines of *lol you stupid bitch come meet us!* But I wasn't fortunate enough to know what I wanted to do with my life post-graduation. Or rather, I knew what I wanted but had no idea how to attain those goals, and so instead panicked myself into a life spent behind a desk. Had I realised this would be it for what felt like forever, I might have spent a few more years sat bare-assed in Old Street station while waiting for the last train home.

I later realised that while 9 a.m. to 5(.30) p.m. was in all senses the 'real world', I didn't particularly like it. I longed to get out and frolic in the open with chump change and a general lust for life, but in the long run this was likely what was best for me.

In hindsight, finishing at 5.30 p.m. was probably a blessing, as the average working day only became longer and longer as I progressed through my career. 9 a.m. to 5.30 p.m. became 9 a.m. to 6 p.m., and 9 a.m. to 6 p.m. soon became 9 a.m. to 6.30 p.m. Ugh. I was giving up more and more of my time for roles I wasn't gaining anything from. The millennial curse of money vs. dreams. Do you pick the job that pays you enough to live, or gives you enough time to chase your dreams?

One thing my first real role gave me was time to create. Though I didn't particularly like the job, I still worked my ass off learning the ins and outs of the company. Within a month, I'd become so good in my role as marketing assistant that I was able to complete all tasks by 11.30 a.m. I remember my boss saying that I should 'stretch out my tasks' throughout the day to keep myself occupied. But stretching tasks that took two hours to complete over the course of an eight-hour working day seemed pointless. Soon enough, my boredom sparked creativity, and I began utilising my downtime at work. And there was a lot of it. Each day after completing my allotted tasks, I'd pull up a work template and write shitty blog posts. In my head, this was a loophole so I could be paid for writing whatever the fuck I wanted. I wrote about my dating life, divulged my fears and insecurities, and sometimes I'd even brave an outfit post.

Eventually, I fell back in love with writing – so much so that the lack of challenge at my day job filled me with dread. I stopped getting up on time, I started showing up late to morning meetings, and ultimately I just didn't give a toss anymore. This was my indicator that it was time to move on. Due to my nonchalance towards the job and the company as a whole, when I was asked to stay on in the role, I politely declined. I had a deadline for my goals, and was so inspired by my own website that I didn't see the role as part of those goals. Instead, it felt like an obstacle. So I quit my job at the world's most boring company and went back to interning, turning my efforts to PR and influencer marketing instead. It was then that I acquired a mentor by the name of Rosalind, and worked alongside her for the best part of four months.

Though it wasn't a paid role, I never felt like an intern; I always felt like a part of her growing company. My voice was heard, and I was introduced to some incredible people during that time. But the reality was I wasn't getting paid, and my last paycheque from my days as a marketing assistant was only going to stretch so far. Like all good things, the internship soon ended, and it came time to look for a real job again. Parting with a boss I adored in search of a paid vocation was a heartache, but we both agreed it was for the best and Rosalind championed what she said would soon be my upcoming successes. With her encouragement and confidence, it only took another month or so before I was employed in a job that, you know . . . paid me. Yay for me, right?

CRY ONLY WHERE THE £££ RESIDES

With a fair few corporate roles under my belt, I'm no stranger to work-induced stress despite the fact that I've frequently mentioned on my resumé that I'm not only proficient in well, everything, but 'work well under pressure'. I low-key lied. Time and time again, I've had to shelve my upset and disdain, saving all the tears until after work. My workload often exceeded contracted hours, and I found myself nodding in agreement to extra tasks, all the while crumpling up old to-do lists to make way for new ones in a rather panicked fashion.

The notion of storing up tears until work was finished is not one that was unfamiliar to me. As a Londoner, I understand first-hand that seeing someone cry on the Underground means don't even fucking look at them, so it became the perfect main-charac-ter-development scene for 'I hate my job' tears. With its spacious carriages, I discovered that the Metropolitan line played the perfect host for post-work stress. Burying my head in one of the free tote bags I'd acquired from events, I found comfort in the routine of

154

crying just to cry. This would be the scene in my Hallmark movie where everything seemingly went downhill but soon enough it would perhaps . . . maybe . . . get a *little* bit better?

With a routine of tears at 6.45 p.m. down to a T, soon enough my post-work cries were no longer the ticket and served little purpose. Upping the ante, I was taught the art of 'crying on company time', wise words given unto me by the same person who suggested getting paid to take a dump was a genius idea. And here's where I was taught this harsh lesson.

At twenty-two, a recent graduate and excited to explore the world of media, I managed to get a job in PR. Yep, this was the first paid role after my incredible unpaid internship. Unbeknownst to me was what it would actually entail, as I barely even knew what PR stood for beyond its use in what they now call 'influencer marketing'. However, what I did understand was that I'd have the opportunity to write and meet incredible people. In my head this meant that it would soon lead me down the path to journalism, and this was the avenue I so desperately craved.

Up until this entry-level role, the extent of my limited PR knowledge had come to me courtesy of the only course I actually attended in my second year at university. Likely entitled 'Public Relations 101: And Some Shit', it consisted of repeatedly being told what *didn't* constitute PR, but never what did. Needless to say, my grades reflected the withering interest I had in the subject matter.

Public relations to a recent graduate, however, meant that morning coffees from Pret were an exciting new realm, and it screamed professionalism to little ol' me. Although I worked in a prominent area for media businesses and small companies, I knew not of the impact this company would eventually have on my mental health – nor my sudden change in vocation in the future.

On my first day, I was asked to cold-call publications in an attempt to get one of our clients' achievements in the press. As you might imagine, this task filled me with dread. Horrified even at the idea of talking to strangers on the phone in my personal life, doing it for work felt like a test for entry to either heaven or hell. It stopped me dead, and my body itched all over. An anxious babe with an inability to converse with people at the best of times, I hadn't considered that my role at this company would involve anything more than emailing faux grievances for cancelled meetings and the occasional meeting room set-up. At least, not on my first day. Still getting to grips with how to use a coffee plunger without scalding myself, it felt like a lot of work.

As with every job I've ever had, it only took me about a month before I was the golden retriever of my office. Perfecting every element of my job spec, I made sure to excel so I could move into the next phase of my career, and I was more confident than ever that my working hard was the way to do this. Naivety was key to the standard of optimism I held myself to in my early twenties, but I would later realise I was simply working harder and exceeding expectations for someone else's personal gain. Doing the jobs of two full-time staff members and working well beyond my means, it only took three months for me to lose all enthusiasm and the motivation to keep going. Routinely ridiculed and talked down to, I no longer felt like one of the team, and by now the high staff turnover and abrupt exits made more sense.

Still, determined to stick it out and see something through for once, I bided my time and stayed, while my partner at the time, John Doe 2, watched me wither away to mere bones due to my anxious stomach and an inability to digest any food properly. In just a year, I'd lost an insane amount of weight, developed severe anxiety, reduced my sleep and cocked up a variety of friendships due to a ridiculous working schedule. One which would see me, the youngest member of staff and only one level above the interns, as the last one in the office each day. As always, I was open to new challenges at work and strived to be good in any role I took up, but this job was proving to be one of the weapons that God said wouldn't prosper, prospering against me. Unsure of my next move, though I despised being there and any mention of work would induce a panic attack, I refused to quit without having another role lined up. Sometimes, however, life comes at you fast.

Spending many of my lunches locked in the downstairs toilet and crying at the passive-aggressive comments given unto me by the woman I was PA – and then EA – for, I saw no benefit to crying on company time anymore. Even after hours spent crying at the local Pret nearby, I was unable to shake the feelings and instead internalised and took them home with me. Feeling utterly worth-less at the hands of my secure day job, I complained mercilessly to my peers as I desperately needed a way out, and fast. The time soon came where I couldn't take the mistreatment any longer.

There's always a breaking point when it comes to terrible work-places, and mine came when the firm hired an outside candidate instead of simply promoting me. After all, I was doing his job and my own. The Christmas party came around, and news came of this new hire in the position that I had been vying for, and I heard through the grapevine that it would be in my best interest to train this plucky junior whatever-the-job-was. Despite voicing my concerns about being a level below this new person and having to train him, I was met with shock and gaslit into believing that this would of course not be the case – until two months later, when our newbie started, I was asked to train him for the job that I worked myself (literally) to the bone for.

After complaining to my boyfriend, I said enough was enough and handed in my notice. It wasn't being told that I was only allot-ted two sick days a year, nor that I should go to the dentist and the doctor in the same one-hour slot so as not to inconvenience the other members of staff. Nor was it my boss misreading the meeting location detailed extensively on email and shouting at me in front of the entire team. What I drew the line at was training someone who, by contract, was at the level above me.

Crying where the mula resides only served me for so long – and also, I had no tears left to cry. Despite having handed in my notice, the three-month notice period meant that I was forced to work with a group of people who resented me for quitting in the first place. Despite their denial of this being the case, I was still made to screen the emails of the woman I was personal assistant to and saw it all pan out first-hand. I had access to a series of email threads detailing my sullen mood and inability to be my usual chatty self with my colleagues, and every letter in this chain felt like a nail in the coffin of my self-esteem.

Though, to be honest, I probably shouldn't have read those emails. GDPR rules aside, reading these emails that transitioned from content pertaining to our jobs to jibes about my well-being made me feel worthless. Bringing me to tears, I felt hated for putting myself first, and struggled to navigate this feeling.

At the time, my boss spent every day trying to convince me to stay, and would use the promise of a promotion to keep me onside, but my mind was made up. I needed to free myself from a toxic work environment, and I longed to be able to stay up past 9 p.m. when my boyfriend spent the night, instead of falling asleep mid-conversation due to sheer exhaustion. I was miserable. A shell of myself, I took some time to figure out my next move and the steps I'd need to be a fun person to work with once again.

THE TEMP THEN, THE TEMP NOW, THE TEMP FOREVER

Being an adult is just fabulous until you realise that the only real perks are being open about your sexual preferences, watching 18+ films and no longer being labelled a bocat or headmout because both labels are socially acceptable now. However, with adulthood – and it's something we likely should have been taught early on in life – comes the notion that you have to work if you want to do things, have nice things and pay for things. Still aghast at the fact that we have to work for a living – and mostly just to cover our bills – my friends and I frequently spend our days complaining via WhatsApp and talking about packing it in to start a more lucrative business. Though business ventures would make more sense if we had access to Bill Gates's millions, and not the mountains of student-loan debts we're hiding from.

My best friend Clare and I have a plethora of business ideas we wish to begin together. Listing different lines of work we might have a better chance of tackling, these conversations capture our excitement but there's nary a follow-through. From a wedding-planning business to podcasts, and simply becoming famous by happenstance like the seventeen-year-olds popping up on our TikTok 'For You' page. Our dedication to relieving ourselves of our menial day jobs and instead working on things that fill us with joy is the focus of our conversations on a daily basis. Between commentary on potential willy and ASOS dress options, we declare that perhaps today will be the day we finally upload something to the business-idea Instagram account we secured the @ for six months prior.

While the ambition to begin these ventures is deep-rooted within us, our follow-through always dwindles as we continually convince ourselves that tomorrow will be the day we start our plan – and then tomorrow is sixty-five days from now. Desperate to wake up every morning and love what we do, we're also realists who know we're perhaps not built for entrepreneurship – and this keeps us from being the Jackie Aina of each industry we long to dominate. With a splash of realism and pessimism mixed in a bowl, like we're making the Powerpuff Girls, Clare and I convince ourselves that perhaps next week – when we have exactly the same amount of free time – will be the perfect time to begin our plans.

Knowing that you can't pay for holidays with Monopoly money and kind thoughts, it was time to do the grown-up thing and get a kinda-sorta job after the worst PR job of my life. Kinda-sorta, because it was evident I wouldn't have a job I enjoyed for quite some time. Still riddled with anxiety by the events of my last full-time role, I struggled to attend interviews because of an inability to pitch myself. So instead, I recruited the help of a temp agency for the time being. This was the first step in rebuilding my confidence. In my head, if I could do a mundane job and, you know, fucking talk to people face-to-face, then I could conquer the world. Not only that, but not having to interview for a role meant that each job felt like a cheeky get-rich-quick scheme.

The first temp job I took on was as a favour, in a Twinings tea store. Yep, they have an actual store. I thought it was fate, because although it was retail and torrid flashbacks of being a teen on the shop floor flooded my memory bank, I was working with tea. This meant that my hobby was essentially my part-time job, and the free cups of tea helped to quell any pre-winter feels. In my short stint at Twinings, I was able to re-adopt a charming personality and lure customers into purchasing teabags that were likely on sale at the Tesco nearby. The 300-year-old building fascinated me and played host to the scene in my imaginary film where everyone struggled to get their dreams off the ground, including my new colleagues. It was further proof that I wasn't alone in this world and that, sadly, we were all creatively stricken in our attempts to make our own 'fetch' happen. Props, Gretchen.

Later, that favour of standing all day at the historical tea site would be enough to land me a job on the front desk at Hearst – or as I call it, Mecca. My *Running in Heels* fantasy was on track to becoming reality, and my lady parts tingled at the mere thought of it.

When I first entered the Hearst building, I could barely speak. Though I wasn't yet where I wanted to be, I was *in* the fucking building and I couldn't believe it. Being signed in and on the books meant that I could roam the white-walled halls, stroke the desks of the editors I stalked online, and perhaps even go viral for having directed my own Hearst elevator-music video.

It was only my second shift when the then-*Elle* accessories editor Donna Wallace walked past my desk. Having envisaged seeing her in real-life before, I already had our interaction completely mapped out, with conversation starters, anecdotes and even the direction each of our heads would fling as we cackled at my self-deprecating jokes. I was going to put my perfect plan into operation: please can I work here? The reality of our meeting, however, was far less glamorous, and the reason was that I'd misjudged one key element: I was a total wet-wipe stan girl. Usually the life of the party, my role at the time was played by the timid geek who gets a makeover and becomes super popular . . . but not until later in the movie. When Donna walked past and smiled in the direction of the reception desk, I immediately cowered as though I'd bumped into an ex.

Needless to say, it took well over two weeks and a series of solo pep talks before I grew the courage to simply say good morning. Coincidentally, that was the very morning she complimented my outfit – and again, like a schoolgirl with a crush, I cowered, but I wasn't ready to admit defeat. It was time to stop pussyfooting around; I'd been given a Willy Wonka golden ticket and had yet to use it. It was time to approach her desk and speak to her face-to-face; however, I forgot four key things:

1. That she's intimidatingly stunning.

2. She's likely very busy.

3. Her dress sense is insane, like *insane*.

4. I hadn't actually prepared anything to say.

Up in the lift I went, shooketh but ready. I walked up to her desk with conviction, looked her in the eye and said it, the three words I'd been struggling to get out for two whole weeks: 'Hi, I'm Lauren.' Much to my relief, she looked up from the mountains of paperwork at her desk, smiled at me and the conversation flowed. I complimented her, she complimented me, and just like that, she restored my dream that someday I'd have my name on a real byline. I suspect she doesn't know how much that seven-minute conversation inspired me, but it did. I mean it really, really did. I immediately rushed back to the front desk with a cheesy grin on my face, all too proud of myself for simply saying hi. I was exactly where I needed to be, despite the many, many setbacks.

THE MYTH OF THE GIRLBOSS CEO

I've been thinking about this for a while – and I'm hoping that someone, somewhere, will remember this, if I detail it well enough. If you're old enough to have been a Myspace user when the website was at its peak, perhaps you'll remember that one Bluetooth guy who dominated the social platform. The black British Tom, if you like. In keeping with the theme of his name, Bluetooth, and his overall branding, his blue profile and perfectly curated graphic feed featured on everyone and their mum's Myspace profile by way of their Top 8. Should you be his Myspace-mate, you may have been afforded the opportunity to become a 'Tooth'. Combining your likely very cringe tag name with the butt end of his, your profile would include 'tooth' after being afforded this honour. For example, I'd have been referred to as *DreamzTooth* if selected to be a part of this elite online crowd. I will neither confirm nor deny my affiliation with the online posse. It caused confusion and intrigue, and you were mostly curious as to why everyone suddenly had the word 'tooth' in their username but pretended you knew exactly what was going on so as not to sound clueless.

This online movement, long before the emergence of girlboss collectives, would be the first level of exclusion on social platforms. But experienced on a smaller scale than today as a friends list of over 100 people was enough to get you into the online inner circle. Not being clever enough to transition these lessons into how we use online platforms now, we really could have used our two-thou-sand-and-slew knowledge to better navigate exclusion vs. inclusion online today.

Though I adore the fact that we've come a long way from women not being allowed to vote and being stay-at-homemak-ers, there are still some not-so-great things about women in the workplace. While sure, the Michelle Obamas of the world make us proud to be women in the workforce, there are those who make you question how they made it to the top. Oh yes, by crushing the souls of the women they refused to help along the way, and wearing this badge of honour like the Infinity Stones of Thanos's Infinity Gauntlet.

I've got a lot of adoration for many women in my field, looking to them as models of who I want to be in five years. I love seeing examples of powerful figures, because it feels more like an attainable goal. Although they say sometimes you shouldn't meet your heroes.

When I talk to friends about some of the worst jobs I've ever had, it always comes down to the managers and bosses I've had who have treated me like shit, whether it was my godawful PR role, where my manager routinely brought me to tears with her cut-ting words and mood swings, or racist women managers and their microaggressions – like calling me 'aggressive' as a means to take me down a peg or two, ignoring me when I was proposing good ideas or straight up claiming my hard work as their own.

The emphasis put on women being a success in the workplace doesn't seem to take into account the fact that a handful of them are actually really terrible people. Not wanting to give up their spot at the top, all too many refuse to extend a helping hand to the little people desperately trying to make it to the next step in their careers.

While they pretend they're carving out a safe space for women in male-dominated spaces, one of the problems with some women CEOs is their approach to fresh meat. The #GirlBoss empowerment movement does little to actually empower women, and instead glosses over the massive imbalances in power structures. Originally coined by Nasty Gal entrepreneur Sophia Amoruso in her debut memoir *#Girlboss*, which I bought and low-key enjoyed at the time, what was once just a book title would later turn into an internet phenomenon that saw women fake-supporting one another as part of an online movement. There were a number of GB-themed events and the term was even listed in job descriptions (ew), but this new wave in encouraging young women to fulfil their greatest potential only looked good from the outside. The reality was anything but. Unlike actual girlbosses reminiscent of Cruella De Vil, who feared young women would squander their potential, women in the workplace used this term as a call for empowerment but there was no real substance behind it.

Trying to keep up with my peers, I truly believed that being part of a woman-led company would be intrinsic to my growth – bringing me one step closer to becoming the boss bitch I dreamed of being. Looking to my managers and account directors as something of a goal, I realised quite quickly that they wished for me to succeed – but not so much that I would excel and move on from them. Cutting me off at the source, these powerful figures would raise me up just enough to believe in myself and then silence me when I was confident enough to believe I was ready for bigger, better, more exciting opportunities. I've encountered a number of women bosses who extended the grace of a helping hand, but not enough to pull you up on to the boat. Lending a finger or a half-deflated life jacket, these figures often used the ideal of you having to do it all yourself in order to get to the next level. A level unattainable without their grace.

In a ten-year span of not knowing what the fuck to do with my career, much less my life, many of the jobs I despised the most were because of a toxic work environment. And more often than not, because of a powerful woman working at the top. This is not to say there aren't women who are powerful, successful *and* nice – there are obviously examples of great bosses who inspire and uplift their employees. Often, when I look back at the jobs in which I thought I'd learn from a role model, I'm crushed by the memories of utterly hating my working environment and staying in it only for the money.

Despite creating an online world dedicated to a new culture of empowerment in the workplace, a number of CEOs were criticised for allegedly building toxic, uninviting spaces for their staff. With a millennial-pink overlay, we were led to believe that it was a 'feminist' movement, and more than just a reapplication of matte lipstick to incredibly chapped lips. It seems to me that the pretty pink infographics glossed over the same issues present at work, but its pale-pink aesthetic lessened the blow and the marketing-led programme distanced us from any real work being done behind the scenes.

I TRAVELLED SEVENTY STATES

True to my idol Solange, the idea of escapism as a means to start afresh is often rampant in my mind. Having tackled the root of my anxiety and come to terms with my loneliness, I was ready for the next step in *BECOMING* (word to Michelle Obama). They say you shouldn't move as a means of escape, but only once you're fully ready. Because no matter the place, your problems will still be present. Perhaps just in a different time zone.

During my childhood, we'd go for six-week-long trips to Canada, staying with my grandparents in Montreal, and we'd often explore the US as a big family holiday too. Travelling from a very young age, and frequently without my parents, my brother and I were afforded VIP access. Wearing our navy-blue T-shirts with the words 'VERY IMPORTANT PERSON' sprawled across them in thick gold-tone lettering, we were always at the front of the line and held the hands of the British Airways staff as we boarded the plane. Independent from a very young age, these long-haul trips to Canada set a dangerous precedent for my desire to travel. Getting used to the comfort of a plane and the foreign sensation of turbulence and ear-popping, I never felt a fear of flying and quite looked forward to the hours spent undisturbed in my assigned window seat.

Yet the notion of one holiday a year grew tiresome, especially as we always headed back to the same place. While my best friend and her brother travelled to LA, New York, Antigua and the rest with their mother who was a stewardess, my brother and I flew back each time to Montreal, where we sweated out our Sunday best in the hot summer sun after church. I longed to travel the world with friends and awaited the time I'd be able to do it, much to my mother's dismay. Her worries were understandable, as we saw young women go missing on a weekly basis, and she was only given more backing when *Taken* detailed sex trafficking in cities I listed I'd liked to travel alone to.

Though I'd been on holiday many times before and technically alone, it wasn't until I was twenty that I truly travelled alone for the first time. Without my older brother as a safety net, I journeyed to the South of France to visit a friend who was studying abroad there. This pivotal moment opened my eyes to a whole new world, as although I was ignorant of the language and prefaced every conversation with '. . . *English?*' I was enamoured by how beautiful it was to see something other than London's abundance of office blocks and dreary grey skies. This short break, which lasted only four days and cost less than £50, started me off on a trajectory that would see me travel on short European breaks three to four times a year.

With travel as a means to reset for me, I was always at my happiest when exploring other cities. This makes me sound like the black British Christopher Columbus, I'm sure. At age twenty-two, when I snagged myself a boyfriend (shout out to John Doe 2) who adored travel as much as I did, it meant I had a designated person to explore the world with. We ventured every-fucking-where and documented it along the way, bothering the world with my travel blogs until we ended the relationship when I was twenty-five. However, by then, travelling had become my identity.

Until age twenty-six, travelling for me meant exploration and a break from the pangs of day-to-day adult life. Mini-explorations of European cities meant mindful weekend escapes and navigating new terrain. Used primarily to refresh myself ahead of another week of painstaking full-time work, these expeditions fulfilled my need to get away and/or forget my existence for a brief moment. Via £13 flights to Scandinavia, I was able to curb the feelings of dread drummed up by secluded office life.

It has always been one of my greatest desires to live and work abroad. Whether it was going to Barbados to fulfil my dream of sponging off of family members and slumming it in the sun, or moving to New York to become a high-powered business bitch, my dreams always stretched far beyond London living. With my mother having grown up abroad, my grandparents moving from the West Indies to the UK, and my stepdad, ironically, also previously living in Munich (the city I currently call home) at my age – it was always on the cards for me. I imagined that, unlike Lauren of *The Hills*, I would *not* be known as the girl who didn't go to Paris. Following my upward trajectory from anxious intern to kind-of-have-my-work-life-together, I found the courage in myself to finally take the plunge. To pack my shit up and trial the life of a Brit abroad.

With true dumb luck, I spoke it into existence. I said to the universe that now was the time for me to move abroad and try this adulting thing everyone was consistently going on about. Within days I received a call via a recruiter on LinkedIn about a copywriting job opportunity abroad. Having recently finished up my role at a newspaper in the UK, I was more than ready for a new challenge. Watching my predecessors succeed in their various chosen countries while meeting the loves of their lives and renting fancy apartments that were a far cry from my London reality, I wanted what they had. I could no longer bear the thought of being the freelance 'not a writer' who just had careless fun anymore; I craved more. What with my peers becoming full-time teachers, accountants and international DJs, I was more than ready to begin my own success story. Despite the Monday morning post-brunch debriefs at the office, my professional life lacked the 'eau de parfum' energy I gave off via my social profiles.

Admittedly, just before the big move, I was at a point in my life where I had no ties to London other than my obsession with seafood boil and of course my very best friends who I'd spend whole weekends with. At that point, I felt I needed an experience that would help me to grow from the stagnant mess I was a part of – starting every week with a bad decision and regretting the outcome come Sunday evening.

Though my dreams were a little further left I took it as a sign that Munich was exactly where I needed to be. The power of manifestation worked hard to keep me sane in 2019, and I was more than happy to take it up on its offer. But with such short notice, this move plunged me into panic mode as, despite my excitement, I was terribly anxious about it all. Where would I live? How would

I communicate? What did this mean for my current situationship? WOULD I GET *LAID*?! Each of these questions plagued me, and I wondered if I was making the right decision after all.

Resistance was futile. Every day that I spent excited about my big move to Germany was followed by a day spent crying after an unprovoked panic attack. But, desperate to prove to my parents that I could do this, I was determined to go on, pretending that my perfectly curated Excel spreadsheets meant I was more than ready for this drastic change. Reliant on my parents for things like rent-free housing and lifts to the nearest Underground station, it was time to attempt the adult thing for real – beyond paying my own bills and working for a monthly paycheque.

The next few days were spent sweating and anxiously pacing up and down my parents' three-storey home, in an attempt to convince both myself and them that I was capable of such a big move given my history with change. Often clouded by my rocky relationship with my anxiety, I wondered how I might survive, and as the days edged closer, I felt sick to my stomach. While I'd love to pretend the story and transition of moving abroad was an easy one, similar to Sheldon in *The Big Bang Theory*, I don't handle change well at all.

Growing up, I always thought of myself as somewhat of an unlucky candidate, and this led me to believe that good and exciting things would only happen to me if truly terrible things were to follow as a reminder of my unluck. It's the reason I'm hyperbolic and sabotage romantic relationships, and why I'm reluctant to pitch to publications regularly. So although I was keen to live and work abroad, I was terrified that it either would not happen or would fall apart at the last hurdle.

Once I finally made the (un)smooth transition, I was a little lost in translation and forced to relearn aspects of the working world – including commuting via a new German-standard method. My life-style in Germany was vastly different to my former life in London, and that fast-paced London life soon became a distant memory – and running for packed Underground trains became a thing of the past. As someone who was used to late-night trips to the Big Tesco and grabbing wine just before Tesco Express closed at 11 p.m., I struggled to adapt to new terrain. Accepting that if I wanted snacks and wine I had to be in the mood for it by 6 p.m. or it would simply not be a possibility was likely the hardest adjustment of all time.

I've certainly indulged in the overall allure of an abroad lifestyle, despite the often-perverse weather conditions in my new city. For one thing, I've acquired some incredible friends, located saucy bars to drunk-text friends from, and Munich is the turning point in my life where I'm finally getting my act together.

Moving my whole life abroad left me open to learning how to better tend to my relationships back home, as things like FaceTime calls became my main method of communication with my friends. The stress of a mundane life is ageing us, experiencing these adult changes that require us to think more about rent and next steps than the parties we'll attend and what to wear.

Living in Munich, I had to adapt and adjust to my new surroundings. While waiting twenty minutes for a bus might seem miniscule, in London it felt like a punishment for my leisurely walking pace. With all shops closing dead on 8 p.m. and the lads on Tinder and Bumble typically sporting traditional lederhosen in their profile pictures, it's a far cry from the world of fuckboys and late-night *U up?* texts from exes I'd become accustomed to in my London life.

Moving to Munich felt like going back to a time period when bus tickets were printed on pink paper, available at 40p a pop, and you always had the option of pleading with the bus driver if ever you were slightly short of change. Living abroad can be incredible, but it bears remembering that it does have its pitfalls, and not seeing your loved ones often is definitely one of those (no access to Caribbean cuisine is an equally harsh pitfall). I spend many of my days navigating life in Munich with the same vigour as East Londoners attempting Spanish with a cockney accent. That is to say, I sound terrible when attempting to say anything more than 'card please' at my local supermarket.

Everyone I meet in my German journey wonders why I selected such a quaint and quiet place, but having only really moved for work, I never have a particularly structured answer. Calling it home now, I never would have thought that my life would revolve around a quiet Bavarian city that focuses on a typically meat-based cuisine. Transitioning from a world of wines after work, beer is the beverage of choice here and my growing beer belly agrees with our new choice of drink.

During such a big change in my life, I was transported back to the only enjoyable portion of my school years – in 2006, when BBC Three's *Little Miss Jocelyn* was at the peak of our schoolyard conversations. With its skits about black culture, and particularly about first-generation black Britons, this new sketch show captured *us*. Missing out on an episode was like missing out on *Big Brother*'s live eviction on a Friday night. Basically it was unimaginable pain, as you couldn't contribute to acting out skits from the night before. A comedian who managed to capture exactly what it meant to live and grow up in the UK, Jocelyn Jee Esien's grip on our Thursday evenings was a veritable chokehold and we loved every thirty minutes of it.

One skit that always comes to mind is of Fiona – described as a middle-aged woman who works in a predominantly white office. The only black and/or person of colour in the office, her entire personality is based on the fact that no one knows her true identity. That she is, in fact, a black woman. Various black antagonists enter her workplace, which means her façade is always at risk of being exposed. Using a number of clichés for comedic purposes, her approach to being found out and desperately trying to fit in with her white counterparts reminds me of every office job I've ever had – and is a lot like what it feels like to move abroad to a predominantly non-black city. But, I guess, on a much larger scale. Moving abroad poses its own challenges, especially as a black Briton. While I was desperate to experience life abroad, I understood that being black and in another country would come with a different set of complications, and I was routinely reminded of this fact by my parents.

Navigating a language barrier is likely the most complex part of moving to a city in Europe, with coming to terms with low-key racism a close second. At first, I tried my best to ignore the lengthy stares on the U-Bahn trains, until I realised the stark difference between racism in London and racism in Munich, which is that they don't look away!!!! Between this and the countless occasions a rather standard black girl from Britain has been referred to as 'exotic', I'd say casual racism has felt almost like a 'that's just the way they are' thing, and so to avoid it I've shelved my attempts at dating apps and completely steered clear of conversations that include casually racist language at work. That is to say, any conversation that begins with 'Is it racist if . . . ?' sees me quickly bolt through walls, leaving only a Lauren-shaped hole behind.

I always worried that, similar to Emily of *Emily in Paris*, my inability to pick up another language would read as reluctance as opposed to the blinding stupidity of not being able to understand anything in German beyond brief sentences and the words 'prescription drugs'. I have never been particularly good at languages. The feeling of not being able to communicate with the local delivery person or Uber driver became a struggle. Small issues like not knowing where to buy the sugar I wanted for a year, due to the fear of onlookers seeing me use the translation app, were all adjustments and instilled anxieties about feeling like an intruder.

A comfortable work life became the primary benefit of living in Munich. It was the first time in my life where I felt I wouldn't be canned without official notice, and the comfort of having a secure job was like a Band-Aid on the slight graze of being out of my comfort zone. Tales of truly terrible work environments and last-minute redundancies became a thing of the past, as I moved on to this almost zen utopia of a work environment. One where I wasn't penalised for taking sick days I was legally entitled to.

Now that I've worked abroad, I realise the unhealthy attachment we have towards work in the UK – and likely the US, as they have a very similar infrastructure. Instead of simply using our allocated sick days to actually be off sick, we've been conditioned to believe that the not-so-well-oiled machine cannot function without us. Wracked with guilt, we continue working even through our ailments and believe this to be normal. While working through the sniffles might seem as though you're proving your dedication to an institution that cares little for you, what you're really doing is prolonging your illness by giving too much of yourself to your day job. There needs to be an off switch so as to restore the equilibrium of the work-life imbalance.

For over ten years of my life, I truly believed that the more I gave of myself in these roles, the better my work karma would be. But the truth is, it only gave way to further work mistreatment. Becoming the go-to person managers would call to cover a shift, I allowed staff members in authority to take advantage of me in the same way fuckboys did.

I remember taking a sick day in Munich and returning to work the next morning after a day of bed rest. And by 'bed rest' I mean spending the day horizontal while writing detailed product descriptions. I wiped the snot dripping from my nose after each Bottega product, and felt as though designer wear was the cure to my illness. But my British attitude to working made me worry about the inconvenience my absence might have caused. My line manager thought me silly for returning to work after only a day spent at home in agony – and for working throughout, despite being told to simply rest. Still a newbie at the company and unsure of the office dynamic, I was perplexed as to why I was told to go home again and recover. I assumed we were all for capitalist propaganda and working beyond our means.

The guilt I felt for taking time to recharge was far worse than the illness itself. Actually, that's a bold and blatant lie, as I was vomiting through all the crevices in my face. Readjusting to the basic need to rest when feeling unwell, I began re-evaluating how I had previously treated myself when under the weather. I realised that going to work was likely the cause of me relapsing and getting a thousand colds in a week.

Adjusting to a new role that has offered me the opportunity to work from home has added to the way I feel about fully dedicating myself to working when under the weather. Whereas before I'd feel a tremendous sense of guilt if my direct boss didn't see me emphatically pounding at the keyboard, I now feel comfort in knowing that I'm trusted to set my own work hours.

30 UNDER 30

Contrary to popular Twitter belief, I do not believe that our challenging relationship with growing older started on the internet. It's programmed into us from a very young age. Told to us in our favourite childhood movies, in addition to the pressure from older (and *real*) adults, we've long been conditioned about what we're supposed to have achieved by age thirty.

I long to be on an exclusive '30 under 30' list to celebrate the little wins, and I feel tremendous pressure from those online announcements and an anxious fire under my ass. Only, in this scenario, I'm a pig with an apple wedged in my mouth and it's the Twitter elite who are doing the roasting. Terrified of seeing online achievements with an age attached, I live in constant fear of other people's good news that I know will make me feel terrible about many of the life choices I made at a young age. Instead of knuckling down at twenty-one, my only real achievements were waking up without a hangover after a heavy night in Shoreditch, and returning home with the exact amount of money I went out with.

I guess it's sort of natural to envy those who have their lives together at twenty-one? And not at all bitter, like the reimagined Princess Anne in *The Crown* is towards Lady Di. Stuck in the same boat as a number of other twenty-somethings, we're up shit creek with nary a paddle. We're confused as to how to actually get the success before thirty we so desire, as we try to figure out this terrifying abyss known to us as life. I've apparently now reached the milestone whereby I preface every comment on behaviour with 'well, when I was your age' – just like those aunts and uncles who stay in your business for no reason at all.

Living in a constant state of worry that perhaps my efforts directly after university maybe weren't enough to garner me a coveted spot on the *Forbes* 30 Under 30 list, I worry that the constant pressure I place on myself (and the standards under-thirties in general hold themselves to) is more of a detriment than a helping hand. Extending an olive branch, twenty-one-year-old Lauren constantly reminds me via my memory bank that we had fun, and we're glad we had fun. Because while of course I would love to own my own home, while experiencing the acts of sheer stupidity I did at that age it just would not have been a possibility, and I have a plethora of sambuca shots to thank for that.

While we may be told online that achievements with the age of twenty-one attached to them are the cause of our fear of not achieving anything of significance before reaching the big three-oh,

I believe it to be the media that we consume from the day we are expelled from our rent-free, all-inclusive home – the womb. Films like *The Parent Trap* represented what it meant to grow old. As a child, the playful discourse between Meredith Blake and the twins seems warranted; after all, she's older and not their mother and they want to be a family. As children, we get it. However, growing up, you realise she was kind of wronged for simply being hot and dating a dude with kids.

For the most part, Meredith – who dislikes children (with good reason) – is a successful publicist who just so happens to meet a handsome man with children. Her dating partner would be the perfect mate in any other instance, but because of them she is portrayed – as with many women in 1990s flicks – as a raging, ageing bitch. Only twenty-six years old, Meredith is made out to be a villain for being only fifteen years older than Hallie. Through this introduction to Meredith's character, as a child you were grossed out by the fact that she's not much older than a child, while as an adult you're scarred by the fact that you couldn't bag a rich bachelor of your own at twenty-six.

We're now rooting for the women depicted as villainous in our former years, as the Cruella de Vils of the world weren't given the fair chance their onscreen counterparts were blessed with. While we were conditioned to see children and marriage as the perfect end goals – in the case of *101 Dalmatians*, aided by happy puppy families and a grotesque amount of dog maintenance – many of us have grown up and favour Cruella's outlook on life instead. Her career-first view is one I greatly aspire to, despite her otherwise girlboss-ish attitude. In the scene in which she compares marriage to famine and disaster, she is advising women the world over not to waste their talents for the title of 'housewife'. Cruella's opinion on marriage is one of many reasons I take hits to my budding career to heart – I view my career as my children *and* my marriage.

The ideal of having it all before thirty is shared by many of us approaching that phase in our lives, aided by the aunts and uncles who routinely poke fun at us for not yet making full use of our baby-makers or our ring finger.

I completely understand that life past thirty is not a death sentence; quite the opposite. I'm told that 30+ is when all of the anxieties built up in your twenties dissipate and you can really start living life. Yet the coveted positions on 30 Under 30 lists out there only further strengthen the idea that perhaps I should *start* getting my shit together long before thirty. I've always sought comfort in the notion that, if this particular career path doesn't work, I can always try something else. And I can try and try until I really truly figure out what my purpose is. Even after thirty.

Despite the notoriety and the celebrations surrounding the covetable achievement of being listed alongside other talented twenty-somethings, I can't help but feel that I should have found my purpose that little bit earlier.

In addition to the pressure of having a sustainable and internet-noteworthy career, *Broad City*'s character Ilana perfectly encompassed what I think it means to be young and married – aka my biggest fear realised – when she turned down a proposal by questioning why marriage would even be a thing for her if she's still a baby girl. My parents', aunts' and uncles' consistent reminders that I may end up alone, should I not drop my cynical ways and *shudders* let a guy in, only add to the notion that we're supposed to have things set up by thirty. Ready for a cushty seventy years of the same man leaving a fresh roll of toilet paper resting on top of the old tube instead of simply swapping it out.

Friends perfectly illustrated the widespread fear of turning thirty. Listing all the things she should have achieved by this milestone, Rachel Green's list bellows out of the screen at those of us teetering towards the end of our twenties. With children and marriage as landmarks for adulthood, we're inadvertently being told that we too should be worried about having it all together by thirty-five. Up until 'The One Where They All Turn Thirty', the six companions seemed to just be enjoying their lives as young adults with great jobs and inexplicably inexpensive apartments adjacent to one another.

Having seen milestones like turning thirty portrayed in a negative way onscreen has ultimately impacted my view. The fear of getting older and not yet being where I thought I would be is a direct result of my over-consumption of media consumption telling me that thirty is the edge of a cliff with nothing but disappointment and bills at the other end.

The Writer on her Self-Discovery

Chapter 5: The Writer On Self-Discovery

*You've gotta decide where you are in your self-discovery —
are you confused like Violet in* Nappily Ever After, *or are
you fucking off on holiday to relearn yourself via a romance
by way of Stella in* How Stella Got Her Groove Back?

They say you can discover yourself at any age. Though I often
wish I'd been the smart kid who sussed out all the jokes before
the punchline, my own pillar of self-discovery started much later
on in life. Today, I understand that there are a number of experiences you're almost *supposed* to go through in order to find
yourself. We watch films where women in particular discover
themselves, then decide that perhaps the only way to get over
their asshole ex is to travel the world. After all, it's better to cry
on a beach lying under the sun than in the bedroom you used to
sleep in with him, right?

Even if you've never watched the film or read the book, we all
know the pinnacle of discover-yourself narratives is *Eat Pray Love*.
It's exciting, enthralling, and it ignited the idea that perhaps the
boys in our local town weren't the complete picture. It seemed that
in order to find ourselves, we first had to step out of our comfort

zone and discover the world – which, of course, is just that little bit easier for a Caucasian woman in her prime, but I digress.

My own version of self-discovery began a little too late, but it appeared in three stages: grief, acknowledgement and then, finally, rebirth. Mourning the loss of the old me following the breakup that nearly broke me, the first step of grief posed two choices: I could revel in my upset, go deeper down the rabbit hole and reach full-blown depression *or* I could start to rebuild myself and relearn what it meant to love myself, for myself, by myself.

Step two meant acknowledging where I'd initially failed, and committing myself to working on those areas and forcing myself to discover my beauty – both inside and out. Though 2018 was a year of crashing and burning in all aspects of my life, I left it understanding that there are things within your control and things that will never be. It was understanding this and repeating the words 'It is what it is, what it is, what it is' over and over that helped me through the worst year of my life and beyond. I learned that one of the things you can control is how you choose to respond to situations. I suspect many of you are reading this sentence like, 'Okay, duh'. But it's something that I have to remind myself of every day. It works in any scenario: when someone upsets me, when Pret runs out of brownies, when the item I'd like to purchase on ASOS is out of stock but still displayed on the site – all of it.

Sadly, a lot of my knowledge and wisdom comes courtesy of the films and TV shows that I binge-watch and later quote to my friends. So, I'm nothing of an expert. The road to my self-discovery is cobbled with my own personal experiences and identifying the root causes of my anxiety.

Though it took me well over twenty-six years – and yes, I'm counting the minutes, hours and seconds that I spent kickin' it in the womb – I now can't imagine *not* loving myself. The journey to self-love isn't a straight road, and my many obstacles, awkward encounters and pointless romances prove just that. It wasn't until I eliminated every single person from my obsessive thought processes that I truly enjoyed my own company. Today, as with other women, I gas myself up like I imagine Rihanna does before heading out scantily clad, because despite what anyone else thinks of you, you are all the things you believe yourself to be – excluding all short women claiming the tall agenda. All the things you dislike about yourself or your character, you have the ability to work on, whether it be that you're subject to overly emotional tendencies in your friendships (me!) or you have an incessant need to overshare when you're particularly fond of a new friend (also me!).

All the less appealing traits I'd built up a tolerance for – I made it my mission to alter. No longer wanting to be the kind of miserable person muted on people's timelines, I chose to live instead and began to scream from the rooftops about how much I adored myself, even when I may not have believed it. Missing terribly the humorous tit of old, I desperately wanted the earlier Lauren back. After all, making a total bellend of myself was previously my major selling point.

The secret to self-love is locked deep within the lyrics of City Girls' 'Act Up' and Whitney Houston's 'I'm Every Woman' – songs that clash in sound but share some lyrical content. Despite these tracks sounding as though they only make sense together if your playlist is on shuffle, they actually match due to their general spirit of embodying bad-bitch energy. Unlocking the secret to being a bad bitch, and favouring this over being a sad bitch – my 'Get TF Over It' Spotify playlist is second to none.

When Yung Miami raps about her sexual prowess by way of her eleventh bar in 'Act Up', I am reminded not only to believe in my slay, but also that people often want something in you that they don't possess themselves. This self-declaration of bad bitchery is simply Yung Miami reminding the world that she is not to be played with and she is in fact *that* bitch. While Whitney's iconic rendition of 'I'm Every Woman', arguably the greatest empowerment anthem of all time, reminds us that we are all we need to be and more. By karaoke-ingly screaming that we are every woman, we're not only professing self-worth, we're also assuring ourselves that we can do it all. This song, originally sung by icon Chaka Khan, reminds you that you've *been* the baddest and have nothing to regret in this present moment.

And when all else fails, Amy Winehouse's *Frank* is an ode to why men can be idiots and you should put yourself and your orgasms first. To my dearest Amy, still my favourite singer, I say this: thank you for creating a bad-bitch jazz album. And thank you to the individual who introduced it to me at age fourteen. Without *Frank*, I would likely still be crying in my bedroom. Ah, teenhood, eh?

ADULTING IS HARD, AND ALSO, I DON'T WANT TO

I'm having one of those moments, I'm having one of those moments, I'm having one of tho—

I can officially say that I've reached the peak in my life where I don't know what I want to do, who I want to do or how I want to do things. I'm stuck in a rudimentary 'who TF are we today?' state of mind and desperately want out. Though I've been told of the quarter- and mid-life crises many times over, I always thought I'd be so numbed by these points in my life, I likely wouldn't care – and I'd just make an impulse decision like a swift and ill-prepared move to the Caribbean, or purchasing a Louis V trunk with the entirety of my savings. I'm not at either of these points yet, but I am terrified of making the wrong adult decision.

I understand the complexities that come with growing up and ultimately . . . becoming an adult. But I don't think I was ever ready for the reality of it all. For example, did you know when you were a child that bills have to be paid EVERY month? Or were you, like me, only reminded of this when the gas meter ran out or the phone bill was well over the monthly budget? Now I can recount my upbringing and giggle at the arguments we had over whose turn it was to go to the shop and top up the meter while we stood in complete darkness.

My true role model is my mother, who rebuilt her own life post-divorce with two unruly children. Her determination made sure that arguments in the darkness soon became fond memories. Today, I miss those problems, though they seemed far greater looking back. Instead, I panic on a weekly basis about whether or not my phone bill will bounce, because my monthly rail fare is due. I imagine I could have Diddy millions and still contemplate the many ways I'll be poor in moments.

You're now thinking: 'Great point, but what the actual F does this have to do with anxiety?' These things are all part and parcel of why I panic on a day-to-day basis. I routinely complain about having no money, but it's only because I'm terrified to spend what money I do have on frivolous activities. I'm what some people call stingy, but only in writing this am I realising that I'm wholly broke for some people and 'yeah, fuck it, let's do it' broke for others. My pals and I sit and chuckle about how little money we have buzzing around in our cobwebbed accounts. We laugh because, if we don't, we'd cry, and as 2018 taught me, I would still be broke once the tears dried up. So, there would literally be no point in crying. Money is often a trigger for anxiety, because it's so costly to be an adult today. Especially in London. I mean, it literally costs a tenner to take your first breath in the morning.

While my panic attacks have decreased significantly (thanks for da heartbreak, 2018), anxiety will always find a way to creep in. Whether it be mild panic about money and monthly debits, panic that my friends may have choked on their own vomit before they tell me they've gotten home safely, or panic about whether or not I forgot to turn off my GHDs. But my wellness routine involves being kinder to my brain when she's in angst. That means living in the present moment and focusing not on what's to come, but what is for us right now. I call these 'little infinities'.

Though I've been dealing with my paperwork without help for well over a year now, paying rent and applying for bill what-have-yous, I cannot say it's ever been a comfortable experience for me. In filling out a form that would be my ticket to eventual freedom of movement between countries post-Brexit – that is to say, a ticket to see my family and friends back home – I froze. Panicking, I entered *fashion_qween44@hot* . . . then tried *lauriie_x3@hot* . . . No, I was no longer the fifteen-year-old perched in front of the MSN emoticons, clouding the computer monitor with a backoff.

To be completely honest, I didn't ask to be birthed into a society whereby I'm required to work in order to make money.

While I'm aware that I am in a 'good place' in my life, I can't help but express how terrible I feel when I experience even the slightest knock-back. Over my twenty-something years of existence, I've become quite accustomed to being rejected – like the nerd in a typically 90s teen flick. Whether it be not tickling my 'type's' fancy, or perhaps not being the right kind of cool for the 'unfriendly black hottie' girl group, or being knocked back by a job or two – I've certainly become all the more equipped for being ghosted or faced with rejection. This has served me greatly when applying to companies that said they would get back to me in due course, and even more so when my texts are left unread for hours.

With age – and I can say this because I'm in the wrong half of my twenties – comes a number of understandings. The tiny inconveniences we faced in our youth were merely setting us up for the failures to come. Whether it was losing a friend to her first high-school boyfriend, or being told 'no' by your father but 'yes' by your mother and feeling utterly conflicted. Little by little, we learned the art of ethics, about poor decision-making and the feeling of regret – in a nutshell, how to adult.

ROOTS & CULTURE, RHYTHM & BLUES

Incredibly proud of my West Indian heritage, I grew up surrounded by powerful and prominent fem' figures. They taught me to be strong, to never show weakness and to work twice as hard as my Caucasian counterparts. But despite being incredibly proud of my Caribbean descent, I can't help but wonder about many of the ways I've been conditioned to deal with difficult situations that may have negatively affected my view on mental health.

Raised to be 'strong' in the face of hardship, I always felt tremendous amounts of guilt whenever I gave in to a depressive episode. It was anything but strong, I'd think to myself. I was often told to quell my feels, and instead to buckle up and move on – and this affected the way I dealt with problems and the speed at which I dealt with them.

Never an advocate of the concept of tough love, as I am in fact a weak-ass bitch (apologies to Megan Thee Stallion, for I have failed you), I struggle to see the benefits in dissociating from one's feelings. Continually pushing back your feels in order to maintain a strong persona only prolongs the issue and adds fuel to the fire. Truthfully, this concept of tough love has never worked for me, and while I'm sure it does for some people – a lot of people, actually – being told to 'fix up and get on with it' only made me feel worse about not being able to put a lid on my out-of-control feelings. Trying to understand why I wasn't able to just pick myself up and move on has definitely contributed to the anxious way I deal with my issues at present. Succumbing to panic attacks about how to actually deal with the situation at hand, I'm guilty for not dealing with things the way I was taught, which was to tackle them head on without the added theatrics of a mild pre-fix-it breakdown.

Anxiety comes in many forms, from freaking out about where your life is going every morning to getting a new freckle, self-diagnosing and concluding that you have every illness under the sun. I've come to be open about having anxiety. I used to be so ashamed, because I didn't quite know how to even approach a mindset like mine. That was until I realised that ultimately it wasn't going anywhere and I had to deal with that reality. Anxiety was a part of the package deal, and unfortunately I had to grin and bear it as it grew with me. Instead, I tried to wear it proudly like the latest Bottega bag.

A number of people in the black community led me to believe that you should only seek therapy if you are truly on the brink of a mental breakdown, but I'm glad to see that idea has since changed for the better – at least a little. We're programmed to think we don't actually need help and that we're weaker than everyone else if we can't handle the issues that make us crumble. But the truth is, those of us who frequently have anxious thoughts are actually stronger than we think because we have to battle those terrorising thoughts, day in and day out. Imagine your own brain telling you that you're worthless and that your work isn't good enough. That alone deserves a best-performance Oscar for trying to keep your shit together.

PERSONALITY TRAITS AND THE ANXIETIES ATTACHED TO THEM

Granted, I'm not a savvy individual with a flair for fashion and top-tier make-up skills but when RuPaul requested that his *Drag Race* season 10 queens present to the runway their inner saboteur, I felt exposed. In an episode that can only be described as a breakthrough, each drag queen is asked to express the things they dislike most about themselves via a voiceover, all the while strutting down the runway in extravagant drag couture – a triggering episode for those of us posing as our best selves on the net while ultimately dying inside. It was a reminder that many of us experience imposter syndrome and often feel as though we're not doing quite enough. With anxiety routinely holding me by the throat, I was led not only to overthink but also cower from anyone trying to raise my self-esteem by way of compliments on my work and overall being.

As an avid *Drag Race* fan, I can't pretend that this chapter isn't mostly dedicated to the queens I adore and y'know, routinely stalk online. One of my ultimate favourite queens, who I binge-watch via YouTube's *UNHhhh*, is Katya Zamolodchikova. Posing as a Russian . . . well, everything, her comedic drag persona touches on all the campy things I adore in a drag queen. Be it a frankness regarding sex, being gross while being glamorous or an inability to keep random sayings in one's head.

But while I have a heap of Katya-isms stored in my mental library, it was her reappearance in the *Drag Race* world on season 2 of *RuPaul's Drag Race All Stars* that rang truest for me. Providing anxious audiences with words to live by, her return to the screen meant that we had memes to flood our Instagram pages with – and an abundance of them, because she was incredibly open about her anxiety, and usually face-to-face with the two-sided workroom mirrors.

During her stint on *All Stars* 2, she was frank about what had held her back during the series she initially starred in – and it was her anxiety. Whenever I feel the pangs of anxiousness washing over me, instead of crumbling to the floor and crying no matter the surroundings as I once did, I recite Katya's quote about choosing simply not to be anxious anymore because she'd reached a new sense of self. And then I turn to the techniques I picked up in my brief stint in therapy and counselling. You're never too strong to seek help, and I genuinely believe anyone struggling with feelings of intense angst should at least try therapy to help themselves out of the hapless routine of forgetting to shower or change the sheets. Had I not sought help, I suspect I'd still be in a relationship with a man who didn't love me, continuing to be taken advantage of by toxic friendships and crying in the toilets at work every hour on the hour.

Today, and three years out of the anxiety rabbit hole, my go-to anxiety relief comes to me in a few forms, whether it be indulging my overly needy Sims characters, writing my worries out by candlelight or rewatching episodes of *The Office* I've seen a million times over.

Though I may have accepted that anxiety is a part of my DNA, I refuse to let it consume me the way it did in the past. Being broken isn't cute and mascara is expensive – as were the clothes I ripped to shreds because I 'just needed them off me' so that I could breathe. I suspect people don't quite understand what it means to have anxiety or aren't sympathetic to it until they're forced to either be around someone who has it or experience it themselves. Living with anxiety is so much more than simply needing to toughen up in the face of hardship, and it often feels like two little *Osmosis Jones* characters fighting for centre stage in the Zit nightclub. Struggling with self-doubt every day and almost getting used to that numbness is terrifying, but it's the perfect time to seek help. Though I'd never claim to be an expert on it, my only advice to those who happen to be around someone with anxiety is to listen and not call us silly when we've plucked up enough courage to tell you why we're feeling down about our lives and/or achievements. Just be kind.

Wondering to myself what I must have done to warrant harsh critiques when struggling through an anxious episode, the concept of tough love doesn't sit right with me. To me, the concept of tough love is not unlike doing my maths homework alongside my mother on Sunday evenings and being asked time and time again: 'If I have FIVE apples and Johnny takes ONE . . .' It just wasn't a way I was capable of learning, and much of my anxiety in the present day stems from being pressured into answering questions on the spot. In my Year 9 Mathematics lesson, where our teacher refused to let us sit until we'd answered one of the equations projected on to his whiteboard. And given how terrible I am at maths, I'm proof that this approach doesn't work. Either that, or I really am just painfully stupid.

I tend to overthink very simple situations, and my initial reaction is to go nuclear or cower. Only knowing how to panic first and act later, my initial reaction is to freak the fuck out. Writing lists, yet still panicking at the sheer amount of tasks listed in black ink, the relationship I have with typically stressful triggers is one that I'm still learning how to navigate.

Anxiety has been described as 'a feeling of unease, such as worry or fear, that can be mild or severe', and this is often my default mode. The constant fear of the unknown even after reaching new wins is something I struggle with profusely, as I'm always terrified of what's to come. This paralysing fear is the cause of my reluctance to try new things or put myself out there, mostly because it takes me out of my comfort zone.

Therapy significantly lessened this feeling of free-falling, but it is still deeply rooted in me as it only takes one minor inconvenience for me to be back in a claustrophobic box of anxiety. Struggling to find the very easy methods to pull myself out of an anxious patch, I'm still learning how to deal with this feeling without crumbling entirely. During my stint in therapy, after truly hitting rock bottom, I met a qualified woman who quite literally changed my life. Regrettably, though, I still remember being terrified of detailing my depression and anxiety symptoms via email beforehand, and after I hit send I worried they might cart me off once and for all.

Sweating profusely at my first therapy session, my voice cracked when I realised I would actually have to speak about my problems out loud. Up until that point, I had either written my upsets via text to friends – following up with *but I'm fine, don't worry about it!* – or just not spoken about my issues at all. She first asked me the areas I wished to target before asking if I was okay. I wasn't. Although John Doe 2 and I hadn't yet broken up, we were well on our way out and I could feel him slipping away from me. Feeling utterly undesirable, unloved and anxious as he refused to admit the end was nigh, I quite frankly responded to my new therapist: 'Erm, I feel a bit shitty actually.' She asked what my triggers were and I promptly told her that, at that time, everything was. I barely left the house, as I was terrified of experiencing another blackout panic attack that saw strangers comforting me and me having little understanding of what had happened.

By session three I was more than at ease with my new therapist and felt comfortable talking about my soon-to-be-ex's dwindling love for me, my fears of losing my friends in a similar way to how I lost my best friend, and work, because my failing career terrified me. She became my sounding board and, despite unpacking major traumas, I felt the weight shifting from my shoulders.

Through therapy I learned the root of my anxiety – well, one of them – and this lesson came to me via my overbearing need to be understood in my friendships. Having lost my best friend at a young age to a fatal illness, I projected many of the feelings and fears of loss on to the closest people around me. Unpacking this allowed me to understand how my anxiety might have affected other areas of my life as my fears of the future, present and past led me to close off entirely and I was generally scared to let new people in as a result.

When the time came for us to part ways, I inappropriately told my therapist just how much I'd miss having her in my life. To put it simply, she fixed me. I went in broken, jobless and on the verge of a breakup, and emerged on the other side with more self-confidence, a good job that allowed me to write the things I was interested in, and single. And it all happened over the course of six months, and while navigating through a torrid breakup. I couldn't have been more thankful, and felt as though I would be losing a friend after the fact. She mirrored my sentiments and told me that she was incredibly proud of my progress, and I took with me all the helpful techniques she'd provided. I was whole again.

TO PARAPHRASE RIHANNA'S 2006 HIT, BREAK IT DOWN, BOY

Meltdowns are a fairly common occurrence, and while some of us experience screaming, crying and/or head-shaving, others experience mild hysteria like when Mariah Carey made an unexpected appearance on MTV's hit music show *TRL* in 2001. I was somewhere in the middle of these. Unsure of what the fuck to do with my life due to the uncertainty of journalism, I was regularly exposed to a little hysteria.

There are Pinterest boards now filled to the brim with beautiful women who've succumbed to the 'big chop', and this is likely where the second stage of my self-discovery truly began. You see, it's rather difficult not to love yourself when you're quite literally face-to-face with your bare head and all of its defects. With no hair to cover your face, your comfort zone is completely obliterated. Though chopping off my locks was more than simply a dramatic gesture, it sure felt that way. What better way to end a terrible year than to end it with a bang?

Cutting off hair is often where a lot of us are forced to appreciate both our inner and outer beauty, because it's inescapable. Not only can you not go back in a hurry, it forces you to change your perception of yourself and learn via your own scalp what products to use, how to maintain clear skin and how to adopt new make-up routines so you don't look *entirely* like your older brother (like I did).

When I first proposed the idea of chopping my hair off, it was met with disdain, worry and a barrage of 'Okay what's going on? Talk to me' messages from friends. So I chose to do it in secret and ask for forgiveness later. But the truth is, although I felt like I needed a drastic change in my life, it wasn't just so I could start afresh. I simply longed for healthy hair.

Sat in the barber's chair, I was asked if I was 'ready' and before I could utter the word 'sure', there was a razor grazing my scalp. Mission accomplished. I was left with an amateur buzz cut and politely asked him to continue. 'No turning back,' the barber jokingly said as he stared me dead in the eyes via the mirror. I knew what I wanted, it was a rebirth, and this felt like just that. Every time the razor touched my scalp, I cared less and less about what the world thought of my appearance and instead created new rules for myself and a new standard of beauty. Imperfect and unpretty were how I'd felt before my hair was shaved down to the slope of my scalp, but now I felt like a newborn discovering the world for the first time.

Much like the feeling of a new tattoo, I felt born anew. I didn't quite realise it at the time, because once I set my sights on something, I have to see it through, but I was about to eliminate the bad taste in my mouth. After cutting my hair off, I was now exposed to people who commented for comment's sake, a boyfriend who clearly was no longer attracted to me, and a barrage of men from my past who couldn't quite get over the fact that I just didn't have hair anymore. In short, a basket of bad eggs.

The conversations I had with men post-breakup were even more awkward than before, and I was rarely approached on a night out, forcing me to raise my 'all men suck' umbrella even higher. The year without my tresses, which I'd previously worn as armour, was spent toying with the idea of cutting it off all over again just so I could determine which men were in it for my slicked bun and wig looks and which were intrigued by my oddly pale head and niche brand of dark humour. This chapter of self-love forced me to remind myself of my peng, despite my fellow man's resistance to dating the bald-headed bae. It was, in a word, refreshing.

SELF-LOVE, ONE OF THE THINGS THAT SOLANGE IMAGINED . . .

Self-discovery is a tricky concept to grasp. Ultimately, you have to decide whether you'd prefer to be angry at the person in the mirror forever or accept them for all their quirks. I chose the latter, and while more often than not I struggle with the whole self-love spiel, it's all a part of the journey. In my adulthood, I'm finding that there is more than one way to 'discover' yourself. Whether it be travelling abroad on your lonesome, or making new friends, or identifying new things you like, there is no one way to love who you are. With everyone on their own paths of discovery and my own still on a rolling contract, it's best to remember that ultimately it's a series of attempts to prioritise. To find oneself is to find true peace. After all, life is too short to spend it at war with yourself.

I can admit that I lost control of my life and found solace in playing God to the Rae-Parkers in Sims 4. I made sure they were financially stable, had a (huge) roof over their heads, exercised daily and woo-hooed when necessary, which in this household was at every opportunity. By child number four – not to mention the incessant texts from friends telling me to get the fuck off the game – I realised I was a little too engrossed in the Sims world. My obsession was ever growing, and soon enough I knew it was time to get a grip on my own life. After all, my laptop was overheating. Much like my Sims character who deleted her boyfriend because the game modelled real life, I had to relearn who I was and how to be alone all over again. Needless to say, being comfortable with someone for so long only brings with it a doubt in every new encounter. Lawren Rae-Parker the Sim switched up her fit, sent her kids to private school, upgraded her career and moved the fuck on, so I had to do the same IRL.

My previous endeavours in the online gaming world were a real learning curve, and showed that there were consequences to my actions. In what I'd call an earlier version of the Brazilian butt lift (BBL) era, online role-playing game IMVU (In My Virtual Universe) meant you could be sexy online and ugly in real life. Free to be as butters as you were in reality, and create an online character that embodied all of your favourite celebrity characteristics, the game left room for you to be the confident busty brunette you hoped to become in the next few years.

My only real aim in spending hours on this game – described as an 'online metaverse and social networking site' – was to create the pengest characters using all the free attributes on offer. The game had 3D avatars with an enhanced bosom long before Sims mods, and my obsession meant that I spent hours dressing and redressing my character until she looked as far from my own profile as possible.

Then I met fellow gamer Eugene, who was my age and taught me all the tricks of the trade to gather freebies, and was reminiscent of Howard Wolowitz from *The Big Bang Theory*. The creepy virtual world was an enigma to a fourteen-year-old who had only recently stopped playing My Scene dress-up games. My online friendship with Eugene bloomed beautifully, as he taught me everything there was to know about the tricks of the trade on IMVU. Wanting to take the friendship to the next level in order to send me a plethora of cheat codes unable to be sent via the app, my online friend in America added me on MSN – and here's where the relationship came to a grinding halt.

No, he wasn't a forty-year-old man, but I was surprised by the creepy fifteen-year-old pictured in his display photo. In real life he was far from the IMVU character he portrayed himself to be. I had almost forgotten that there were real people hidden behind these avatars and online accounts.

My Sims 4 story also came to an abrupt halt just after my breakup. In a truly catastrophic series of events, I'd been locked out of our joint account and figured saying, 'Hey, I know we're not a thing anymore . . . but could you slide me our Sims password pls, I lost it, heh?' just wasn't the ticket. Struggling to get to grips with real life again, the readjustment process meant filling after-work hours with home workouts and conversations with people in the flesh. Given that rushing home to play with my make-believe life was no longer an option, I had to reintegrate myself into the real world and it felt that much harder the second time around – the first being with John Doe 2 – without my virtual safety net.

The perfect stepping stone to reintegrating back into society and getting over terrible heartbreak, I desperately needed Sims 4 – and the thought of my online family living life without me felt like the second-hardest heartbreak of 2018. Feeling entirely unlike myself, I missed that safety blanket more than my ex, and longed for the comfort of my fake online life. At the very least, in the Sims world I was able to fake a love life I feared attempting in the real world. Uncomfortable re-entering the dating world after having my heart ripped out and flung in the dumpster, it felt that much safer to watch my Sims fall in love in hour-long interactions than to engage in meeting someone romantically myself. Clicking multiple buttons to make my characters fall in love with one another and using cheat codes to help them remain in a happy and healthy union felt much easier than taking in my ex-therapist's advice that 'you have to accept that there are some things you cannot control'. Instead, I forced my characters to stay in love with one another for as long as their timelines in the game didn't expire. My obsession with creating an online world where I could call all the shots helped me to feel as though I had a handle on my life, despite it falling apart when I stepped away from my Mac computer.

Regaining some semblance of control and then losing it all to something as trivial as a changed password once shared between two lovers felt like a real fuck-you to all of my efforts to move on in my own time. Shaking things up, I would be forced to get the fuck out of bed, look myself in the mirror and admit that we were not okay losing the person who we believed to be the love of our lives. As I sobbed uncontrollably at the loss of two lives, real-life Rae and simulated Rae-Parker had to part ways to make way for the butterfly effect that would turn my depressive caterpillar into a self-loving butterfly who don't need no man.

Having to *shudders* socialise despite the anxiety of bumping into the person that broke my heart, I was forced to keep pushing on. Making sure to dress to the nines, I tried my best to make myself feel as great as the characters I'd restyled at every opportunity – while using my very limited resources. Finally, when I started to feel great about myself and the anxiety that I might just run into my ex-boyfriend had lessened, I began to branch out and sought more stamps for my burgundy passport.

Using travel as a Band-Aid on the road to recovery, I travelled to remind myself there was more to life than London, and this helped to distract me from the fact that I was in dire need of my transitional safety blanket. However, now that I've come out the other side better for it . . . again, I can hold up my hands and say that perhaps I needed to be weaned off of the simulated game. Given that I didn't sleep and made tiny versions of each of my friends, it may have been for the best.

During this time, Solange was my safe space. Unapologetically herself, Solange showed me as a black woman that I had the power to be great in my own skin. Her effervescence was a constant reminder that in spite of what people might think or who they compared me to, I had a right to feel fabulous in my own right – slaying in my own lane. Creating whole artworks that are authentic to her brand, the singer and actress truly embodies what it means to love yourself, and it was through the visuals for her EP *True* that I learned how to be true to myself. In colour-blocked suits and vibrant clashing prints, the singer-songwriter declared her sense of self with an album that encapsulated her whole personality.

Bobbing around in front of different scenic 'scapes in Cape Town, South Africa for her video, and standing out against the crowd – as black women often do – Solange dispersed a number of home truths and life lessons. Her hit 'Losing You' deals with losing the interest of her partner and offers sage advice, and I heavily related. Instead of depicting a tale of heartbreak with visuals of tear-filled eyes and a sense of desperation, the playful nature of the video is what really rings true for me. Navigating heartbreak through elevated ensembles and painting the town red in her decorative suits, her determination to go on is how I move on in life. This might not be the video's original premise, but it's definitely my take on it.

With a number of different looks under her belt, the singer's authenticity throughout her career remains one of the reasons I stan her to my core. Never afraid to take risks in her style and with her craft, albums like *When I Get Home* and *A Seat at the Table* are like the soundtrack to my life, as I too am weary of the ways of the world.

Understandably, loving yourself out loud rubs a lot of people up the wrong way. The mere thought of you not hating your stature or your face and instead proudly professing a love of your flaws is a call for ridicule to some. But the secret to self-love is rooted in the self-declaration of loving yourself, and saying it repeatedly out loud. Whether it be via your social platforms or screaming it at the mirror as you *ayyy* your way into a fanciful evening, the secret is in saying it out loud. When I discovered this, I changed my own life. Instead of ridiculing the figure I saw staring back at me in the mirror, I began telling her that she was beautiful and deserving of all the things she desired – whether that be a small sum, to the amount of £50k, or a vintage Louis Vuitton trunk – and the more I reminded myself of my self-worth, the more I began to believe in it.

HELP! I'M A TV CLICHÉ

Two of my biggest inspirations growing up were Betty Suarez and, as you already know by this point, Carrie Bradshaw – fictional characters, but inspirational nonetheless. Though I didn't agree with a lot of Carrie's practices or really her decision-making as a whole, I longed to be fashion-forward, forward-thinking and provocative with my writing. She embodied a number of qualities that I coveted, and so I spent my time tirelessly learning the ins and outs of the characters of *SATC*.

A number of us liken ourselves to Carrie for a few reasons, and one of them is that she lived on what seemed like an endless salary by only writing one column a week. Though she's a shitty friend, her resilience when it comes to the written word is something else. She is all too often inspired by the stories her friends told her over cocktails, and that seems to have rubbed off on me. I'd unknowingly picked up personality traits from this TV show during my early years, when I wasn't supposed to be up past 10 p.m. Carrie, like many of my favourite characters, embodies raw confidence like no other. She is incredibly self-expressive, both in the way that she dresses and in the way that she speaks to men, as though no twenty-something can knock her off her pedestal. Despite her incessant need to be pair-bonded with a male, she makes single life look exciting and a journey of self-love. Simply by attending the cinema on 'date night' on her lonesome, or ordering lunch by herself without a book for comfort – her character gives little nods to self-care when alone-*alone*. I'm actively ignoring the parts of her character that spoke about the sadness of not having a man in her life on her birthday. Because, hey, nobody is perfect.

Betty Suarez's irritating charm and unrealistic good luck somehow spoke to the teen me. *Ugly Betty*, with its endless quotable material, was one of those shows that made you feel, as a hopeful young writer, that you had something to look forward to. Every Friday night at 8 p.m., I'd tune in to *Ugly Betty* and another layer of dramedy would be revealed. Betty's relentless optimism was something I saw in myself, despite my vocal pessimism. Her unwillingness to give up in even the most stressful situations was what led me to believe that writers had to struggle if they wished to succeed – though perhaps not as much as our dear Betty.

Rewatching these two shows a few thousand times over, I now know why I chose writing as a career option. Both characters are so consumed by their passion that they refuse to ever give it up. Except for Carrie . . . that one time she moved to Paris. Passion is something that's driven the three of us. To madness.

These shows are ultimately where I found my personality and, though I didn't know it, they were a part of my wellness routine. After all, my ideal life is what the fifth season of *Ugly Betty* should have been, had it existed.

SELF-CARE & DEM MAN

I've realised that a key part of self-care is being selfish. It's not necessarily a free pass to be an asshole, but it is a pass to being selfish with your time, your mind and the things that plague your mental health. Admittedly, I was once a slave to my friendships and desired nothing but to make sure everyone else was okay, even when I wasn't. Really fucking stupid, right? To channel Regina George in my all-time favourite flick, *Mean Girls*: 'I can't even – whatevs . . .'

If you're anything like I was, then you'll have routinely felt guilty for shutting off and focusing on yourself for short periods of time, whether it be to masturbate a couple (hundred?) times, catch up on the shows that everyone is already a third of the way through, or simply to scream heavy-metal lyrics at the top of your lungs. Though I wouldn't dare answer a text mid-wank in the present day, I have done so in the past to tend to my friends when they were in turmoil, and I just know the spirit of Samantha Jones is judging me as a result. Having only now gone through a period of understanding my own boundaries and just how to be *politely* selfish, I'm learning that there's an art to selfishly caring for your well-being. Because ignoring your needs for the needs of others is what? *Chaldish!*

While 2016 may have been the year of 'realising things' – made notable by Kylie Jenner – 2019 quickly became the year of 'if I want to, I will' – word to the plucky individual who made this phrase viral. We all inadvertently sported our 'give a fuck much' badges and took up a carefree attitude towards our own lives and our upcoming successes. This meant that we raised our self-care flags a little higher and told the world to go fuck itself if it tried to make us sad at being in our own skin. I tend to my feels as though I would my skin post-shower in my (frankly, non-existent?) skincare routine, applying only the products that will benefit me. After all, who wants to get spots for indulging in the brownies they swore they've given up?

Post-realisation of putting my feelings first, my mantras quickly became a series of tweets in support of regular masturbation and selfishly putting one's orgasm before the needs of friends and peers. Genius, really. But self-care isn't simply about achieving a mental climax; it's also about not giving a fuck about what anyone else thinks of you. You're likely now understanding why my self-deprecation is so rife and why I wave the humour flag so high. The answer is simple: happiness.

It bears repeating that in order to be your best self, you must first acknowledge your emotional state and take better care of your mental well-being. Many of us wear our stress everyday like Glossier's priming moisturiser, and a lot of our mental well-being relies on how we treat ourselves in the long run. When I treat myself better, I look and feel better.

Never fearful of speaking up about masturbation, it's probably my favourite self-care method of all time. Early on, I developed a fascination with what it meant to achieve an orgasm or the feeling of real ecstasy. It was shows likes *Sexcetera* – watched well past sleepover curfews with my best friend – that led to a major curiosity about my own body when I was old enough. Discussing everything from fetishes to sex toys, while depicting bodies in the buff as normal, this show opened my eyes to masturbation beyond humping pillows after dark. And so, when I liken self-care methods to masturbation, I feel it's a tried-and-tested method for me. The proof is in the pudding, as when I find the time to rub one out with one of my preferred bodiless boyfriends aka a sex toy, I'm often complimented on my spike in mood or glowing skin after the fact.

Growing up from the horny teen who dry-humped inanimate objects for a climax, my adult life could have only gone in one direction. I *won* my first vibrator at an Ann Summers soiree held at one of my friends' student flats at university. I didn't know what to expect, but I heard the words 'sex toys' and 'lingerie' and, throwing caution to the wind, I responded, 'You son of a bitch I'm in!' A number of games were played to determine the winner of a battery-operated golden bullet, and I of course won every round. My very first, I named him Steve before finding out years later that he shared the same name as my best friend's dad. He was a gentle lover, though he got the job done faster than any man I'd encountered by age nineteen. At this point, and similarly to Charlotte York's introduction to the rabbit vibrator in *SATC*, I knew that my chances of leaving the house were slim. I began to wonder what men's real use was beyond splitting headaches and gaslighting.

Later on in life I went from battery-operated to rechargeable. Scarred by the time Steve the Bullet stopped mid-session, I became less reliant on him and needed a vibrator promotion. And with this upgrade I understood more and more that the secret to keeping a smile on my face was frequent orgasms. Similar to chasing the feeling of success, there was a sigh of relief once each session was over, as my muscles relaxed and I forgot the many reasons I might have been stressed out before rubbing my nether regions. The combination of masturbation and minding my business aided me throughout my singledom, as I was able to alleviate the drama, tend to my own needs and reset my mind frame in the same breath.

INSTAGRAM FATIGUE. BURN OUT? BURN ALL OUT, DID YOU?

social media

/ˈsəʊʃ(ə)l/ ˈmiːdɪə/

A fantasy online world where the bodies are sculpted, the skin is flawless and dreams go to die.

Today, the rule is that it's not happening unless it's online. People need evidence, and why wouldn't they? You share everything else with these strangers – something that I took to heart in the early Instagram days. I remember posting photos of myself crying thick black mascara tears when I was low, licking Lucozade bottles to – well, I don't know why actually – and posting terribly blurred photos of my new Jeffrey Campbell-esque shoes, when Instagram was still young, hip 'n' fresh. Testing the waters, if you like. Back then, I assumed that anything went, seeing as no rules had really been set for this flashy new platform. Instagram was whatever you made it, and if that meant posting blurry photos and calling it art, no one was going to question your already questionable aesthetic. Anything to get those eleven likes, eh?

The same went for relationships on the 'gram; if you had a boyfriend or girlfriend, then fuck it, it was time to get creative on Pic Stitch and show them off in a series of incredibly cheesy snaps, ones you'd likely delete a year into the relationship because the unofficial rules of Instagram had evolved and Pic Stitch was no longer 'cool'. If you just so happened to bump into a fellow 'grammer IRL then you'd fucking take a photo with them, slap the Valencia filter on it and post the sodding thing online. People needed to know that you'd met in real life and confirm that they weren't in fact a Sim.

Over time, things only grew wilder when trendier accompanying apps came into the mix. We were introduced to VSCO and realised that perhaps black-bordered photos weren't the answer to our every Instagram woe. Soon enough, you weren't cool unless you were caught 'cute off guard' posing in front of a deceptively white building, and God forbid your photos looked as though they weren't professionally taken.

The rules for this particular social platform became denser and harder to follow, with fewer and fewer of us fitting into the criteria and many of us struggling to be noticed. Some of us felt like we just couldn't commit to the new Instagram lifestyle, instead craving Facebook-like albums that consisted of every image taken on the family's Sony digital camera. To combat this, instead we'd disappear and later return by way of a fire selfie or a lengthy caption explaining said disappearance.

Today, and with PR and marketing involvement, I find it difficult to be myself online – my authentic self, that is. Although people bang on about wanting to see it all, no one *really* wants to see real lives pan out online. Realism isn't nearly as desirable online as the image of a perfect life and zero problems. I've done it before, and the dwindling likes when sharing something I was passionate about affected me more than I cared to acknowledge. Desiring painterly prints, perfectly curated feeds and the odd coffee JPEG that sparked cravings for the greenest matcha, real life became harder to convey to people who wished I would just STFU about my (lack of) relationship woes on Twitter.

My unhealthy attachment to social media was just the ticking time bomb I needed to detonate in order to reset my self-esteem. Regularly divulging the intimate details of my life and over-explaining my absences, my innate fear of judgement for *not* posting pushed me to overshare with online friends and foes on a regular basis. Getting to grips with a reality outside of my smartphone came with a newfound ability to decipher my ill intentions for engaging with the apps I spent my mornings browsing before starting my daily routine. Resetting my mind frame on what was most important (that is to say, a morning coffee and immediately getting up, instead of an hour-long scroll in bed before my third alarm hit), I understood that it was time to reframe my relationship with the online world that had begun to make me dislike myself.

It's healthy to take breaks from social media and to get to grips with reality. What I often learned from these breaks is that

I was spending way too much time analysing how I was being perceived or portrayed by the people who follow me – and the people who don't follow me, but know exactly how to find my ever-changing handle. On these breaks, I'm reminded that perhaps a few hundred likes on the outfit I'll likely never wear again isn't as big a deal as I make it out to be. Though it often feels like it.

With celebs such as Justin Bieber, Pamela Anderson and Ariana Grande, to name a few, all taking leisurely breaks from social media apps, it's probably advised that you do the same – right? I dread to imagine the kinds of thoughts that frequent their minds, considering mine were only regarding who I might be sleeping with or whether or not I *really* looked like that in real life. (The answer to the latter is 'no', by the way.)

I chewed a friend's ear off – as I always do – about the idea that celebrities and influencers talking about mental health elicits one reaction, while hearing it from us regular-degulars receives quite the opposite. When I first opened up about my anxiety, I recall a number of people who referred to me as 'brave', while the others clicked the unfollow button and switched off from my feed entirely. My likes lessened, my self-esteem crumbled and my anxiety only grew stronger at the hands of an app that exasperated me. Punishing myself, I used their response to my mental-health story as a personal grading system and felt like utter trash for having ever revealed my truth – the reason I'd done so in the first place was because I'd watched influencers share their stories and be praised for speaking up.

Over time, I've come to terms with the fact that social media isn't the be all and end all in life, though it often feels like it is.

SINGLE AND FABULOUS, EXCLAMATION POINT!

I'm of a mindset now whereby I'm not scared shitless to be alone. All of the scaremongering put into me by (real) adults and older family members no longer spooks me, as I've learned nothing can be quite as taxing as the pressure I put on myself to succeed.

We've long been taught that women who are alone are miserable and unhappy. I can only remember seeing married women as fulfilled in storybooks, while their single counterparts remain miserable and in an endless search to find 'The One' (word to Teedra Moses). In Charles Dickens's novel *Great Expectations*, the jilted bride wears her wedding dress every day after being left at the altar. A riveting tale, the story of Miss Havisham haunted me throughout my teenage years. I was led to believe that a wealthy 'spinster', for want of a better word, would be unhappy simply because she was alone; I had great trouble understanding Dickens's actual point. I struggled to get past the idea that this person was her 'one', given the state he left her in. I mean, would your soulmate really leave you on your wedding day if he was in fact the one? Having always desired to be rich and left the fuck alone, I struggled to wrap my head around a story in which a woman felt this low simply because she hadn't a husband. During English Literature lessons, the poem 'Havisham' by Carol Ann Duffy served as an introduction to what it meant to be truly alone, and I would later learn of the fear instilled in women who choose to be on their own.

Though being a single woman is more socially acceptable today, and made so by notable muses like Tracee Ellis Ross and Lizzo, we were taught via great literature that being alone was more embarrassing than actually being embarrassed by a man – and this narrative kept us from learning to love ourselves without the addition of a romantic partner. Lizzo's 'Soulmate' is just the kind of track we needed growing up, to remind young women that although romantic partners make for a fantastic addition to the picture, they are not everything. Declaring that we are the own loves of our lives, we learned through songs like this one that the greatest love is found within. Much like that of Tracee Ellis Ross's character in *Girlfriends*, previously we were desperate to find a partner so we could begin living our lives. It's the way we were conditioned to view adult life, which for women was meant to involve a doting husband, screaming children and being a homemaker who adored her kooky family dynamic.

Though I hate to admit it, I was once a serial dater, enthralled by the mere idea of a man being so enamoured by me that I could woo him with my feminine charm. Okay, well, it never really happened that way, but it's fun to pretend while reminiscing. Routinely checking 'Y' on the box that suggested we date IRL, I was no stranger to enjoying a man's company and trying him on for size. Through cocktail-date disasters, Nando's catch-ups and walks through crowded public spaces, I tried it all and greatly enjoyed the way being centred or fantasised about made me feel. It's that moment when your date seems like an episode of *SATC*, and those first date *feels* kept me going during my early twenties as I routinely chased that high.

But it was after these magnificent dates that I got to grips with what I was really feeling – and that was the feeling of addiction. Much like the drugs we *do not* take, my brain quickly became addicted to the overwhelming feeling of being wanted and desired. Even if only briefly, I was driven by the fact that someone found me attractive enough to spend time with me, and suffice it to say that high drove me to madness. Oftentimes, I humiliated myself in order to merge the image I'd painted in my head with the reality standing before me. Through this high I allowed behaviours that make me sick to my stomach now, like quadruple texting, and I mistook clear disinterest as mixed signals. Mixed signals do not exist; he just doesn't like you enough.

Navigating the dating scene with little sense of how the other party may have been feeling towards me, I continually allowed these meaningless relationships to dictate how I felt about myself. Whether it was seeing the 'upgrade' after dating me and concluding that perhaps I just wasn't pretty enough, or taking miscommunication or a lack of conversation to mean that I must be boring – these were nails in the coffin of my self-esteem.

More recently, in my effervescent singleness, I've come to understand what it means to be both alone *and* happy. Unsure of what I want from my future, whether it be children and a husband or peace, solitude and a puppy, my current driving force is the reminder that I do not like the relationship I have with myself after these interactions. That is to say that dates fill me with dread. I always think back to the beginning of each interaction and wonder what I might've done to change things, when often it's nothing I've done differently. Instead, it's that his brain no longer dings 'green' when he sees my number appear, and instead now dings 'red alert'.

I don't know about you, but I've always been wildly self-critical, particularly in the frame of relationships. My inability to forgive my own mistakes leads my anxiety to wreak havoc on me. My new approach is to enjoy my own company and learn to enjoy these brief encounters when they come my way. It's the little infinities that matter to me now, as opposed to full-scale relationships and the arbitrary rules set in place for them.

I was shaped by many of the songs I grew up gyrating to during episodes of *Top of the Pops*, but few struck a chord with me like those of the Spice Girls. Their hit 'Who Do You Think You Are' taught me the art of being a bad bitch, long before that term was even coined. Begging my parents to purchase me the Baby Bunton doll that looked nothing like Emma IRL, my freakish doll sang a series of one-line lyrics when you pulled at the tab behind her pigtails stating that ambition must be my driving force, while she looked vacantly into my soul.

The song would later become a feel-good empowerment track to remind me of my goals and where I'm headed in the future. But more importantly, it would be one of the many feminist anthems that have shown me how to go it alone.

ACKNOWLEDGEMENTS

Whew, what a ride that was. There are a few people I'd like to thank who continued to believe in my talents when I struggled to do so myself. Each and every one of these people is the reason why I'm reluctantly forcing this biog' down people's throats. Special shout out to Silé, Clare-Bear, Vickums, my mama, Soraya and Sharky for guiding me through this terrifying process. I know it can't have been easy to have snippets rammed down your throat every sodding day, especially given how much shit I chat in the intervals between those snippets. Nevertheless, each and every one of you inspires me and I'm ever grateful that I didn't scare you away during this time.

In truth, this was likely the hardest task I've ever faced in my life. Heartbreaks, friendship breakdowns and a number of ripped skirts aside, digging deep into my life has been a rather cathartic experience and one that I likely will relay in therapy in the coming weeks. An experience that involved me crying an inordinate amount and fixing myself via the bad-bitch method of Whitney H x City Girls detailed in Chapter 5.

My passion for the written word has always superseded my love of anything else, and the loves of my life know this to be true – so when Victoria and Silé placed their trust in me enough to allow my dream to come true, I feared I may let them down (in the same way one might feel after being placed in the higher set for Maths despite showing class-clown tendencies previously). Their trust and faith in my craft have been the driving force behind this piece of work, and for having two such talented women championing me in order to help this confused millennial's dreams become a reality, I am eternally grateful.

Lastly, I'd like to thank my mother, who on our impromptu FaceTime calls reminds me on a regular basis that I am capable of the things I doubt I can do. Your belief in me, though I still struggle to understand it, has always been the uplifting, helping hand I need to raise me up when I reach a particularly low point.

BLACK BRITISH GLOSSARY

Or . . . simply a quick guide to all the gibberish I typed.

backoff [back-awf]
    noun – refers to a large bottom/backside/ass. *Example*: 'She's got a nice backoff.'

bocat [bow-cat]
    noun – refers to someone who engages in cunnilingus, or to go down on a woman.

creps [kreppz]
    noun – another way of saying shoes, often referring to snazzy trainers – or sneakers, as my American counterparts might say.

deeped [deep'd]
    verb – as Kylie Jenner described in her 2016 New Year's resolution, to 'deep' something is to realise it. *Example*: 'I just deeped it, I should be on my period by now.'

five-day pass

noun – what millennials used at high-school level to text and call one another for five days. Costing just a fiver before reaching its inflation level of £7.50.

headmout [hed-mowt]

noun – refers to someone who engages in fellatio, or to suck a willy.

lickadickaday [lick-a-dick-a-day]

nonsense – an incredibly uncool prank played in the early noughties, but also I'm not totally opposed to using this in the present day.

lipsing [lip-sing]

verb – black British slang used in the early 2000s, meaning snogging or making out. See also 'lipsed'. *Example*: 'We didn't do much, just lipsed and he fingered me a bit.'

mufti day [muf-tee /deɪ/]

noun – most schools in the UK are required to wear a uniform, and mufti day or 'own clothes day' is the one day a year where you pay a pound towards a charity of the school's choice and get to wear your own clothes. LOL if you were the one kid who forgot about mufti day.

oldaz + youngaz [olders + youngers]

noun – oldaz is used to reference people even a year older than you who look out for you. Younga is used to describe the protectee. *Example*: 'Oh that's my younga still.'

peng [/peŋ/]

adjective – UK slang used to describe someone or some*thing* attractive. *Examples*: 'This food is so peng.' 'He was *ridiculously* peng, absolutely I would hit.'

ABOUT THE AUTHOR

Photo © 2021, Sara Schlappa

Lauren Rae is a twenty-something black British journalist and writer. Her originally self-published memoir completely sold out in just a few weeks on a limited print run. The demand for a reprint was so high that Lauren created a newsletter combining a love of memes and obsessive TV references with the tribulations of day-to-day life, keeping her readers sated with comic relief, nostalgic reference points and sage life advice.

Lauren is based in Germany, having grown up in the UK with an insatiable wanderlust. Her journalism has featured in *Stylist*, Bustle, Refinery29 and *Elle*.